'Can You Speak English?'

A History of Neighbourhood English Classes

based on the recollected experiences
of some of its members and friends

Edited by Rose Grant
&
Elaine Self

NEIGHBOURHOOD ENGLISH CLASSES
London

First published 1984
Neighbourhood English Classes

ISBN 0 9509302 0 2

British Library Cataloguing in Publication Data

Can you speak English?
1. Neighbourhood English Classes—History
2. English language—Study and teaching
Foreign students   3. Minorities—Education
(Adult) Great Britain
I. Grant, Rose   II. Self, Elaine
371.97′06   LC3736.G6

ISBN 0-9509302-0-2

Additional copies may be ordered
from the publisher at
32 Hillway
London N6
Please send cheque with order

Photoset in North Wales by
Derek Doyle & Associates, Mold, Clwyd
Printed and Bound in Great Britain by
Redwood Burn, Trowbridge, Wiltshire

Contents

Photographs by Henry Grant

For Ruth Hayman

1913 – 1981

She had . . . 'a gift that is given to few of us — an inner vitality, an energy that seemed inexhaustible, a restless eagerness to be up and doing.'

Alan Paton

Preface

Frances Weinreich

This book would never have existed if it were not for two great forces. One was Neighbourhood English Classes. The other, the editors.

To the editors, my heartfelt thanks for their dedication, and my undying admiration for their perseverance and hard work, right up to the moment of publication.

The founders of NEC always hoped, from its very inception, that their activities would encourage local (perhaps even national) government to provide for the English language needs of new settlers in Britain. To a large extent, the wish has become the fact.

With negligible funding, NEC embarked on bold ESL experiments which have now become accepted practice with many local authorities throughout Britain.

Recording our pioneering days is not a luxury. The lessons we learned will be valuable to everyone. How we reacted to changing conditions, how we applied ingenuity to insoluble problems, and how we challenged bureaucracy, and won.

We thank all our contributors for their generous response to our request for personal reminiscences. We apologise to all the students, teachers, local councillors, administrators, doctors, health visitors, volunteers and friends whom we did not ask for their valuable memories. We had neither the time nor the resources and regret the inevitable gaps that must occur in this history.

But from those we did ask, the most persistent refrain was, 'NEC changed my life.' We regard this as the finest tribute anyone can pay to the memory of Ruth Hayman.

Introduction

Rose Grant

In 1976 a survey, *The Facts of Racial Disadvantage*, carried out by Political and Economic Planning (PEP), reported that 'in round figures, 40 per cent of Asian men and 60 per cent of Asian women speak English only slightly or not at all.'

In August 1981, a Home Office Select Committee on racial disadvantage reported that 'language remains the source of disadvantage which could be most readily affected by Government action.'

In September 1981, basing its recommendations on a nation-wide survey of English as a Second Language needs and provisions which it had sponsored, the National Association for the Teaching of English as a Second Language to Adults stated, 'Government has a major responsibility to provide for the educational needs of adult second language speakers settled in this country and must ensure that the necessary policy decisions are made and the funds are available to meet those needs.'

How Neighbourhood English Classes came into being, what it did, the who and the where of its pioneering activities are part of our recent social history. It is a history that encompasses the transition of our society into a multi-ethnic, multi-racial admixture resulting from the arrival here in the 1960s and 1970s of tens of thousands of immigrants, refugees and migrant workers.

The census of 1971 showed that 1,400,000 members of the population of Great Britain were of New Commonwealth origin (the Indian sub-continent, Hongkong, Pakistan, Afro-Caribbean) – that is, 1.7 per cent of the total population.

The 1981 census puts the figure at 2,200,000 – 4 per cent of the population.

Men and women among the new settlers who did not know English and could not communicate in it often found themselves at a grave disadvantage. Local initiatives to offer them tuition in basic English sprang up in scattered concentrations of need. Neighbourhood English Classes was one such initiative which proved immensely effective.

We began in north-west London with two daytime classes run in conjunction with Camden Community Relations Council. By the end of 1978 NEC had grown to 120 daytime and evening classes in ten inner and outer boroughs of north London* as well as in Watford and Luton to the west. There were 83 NEC teachers and 30 volunteer classroom assistants, and child helpers were helping in 30 classes. NEC was actively associated with the inception and running of five home tutor schemes through which about 300 volunteer tutors were giving English-language practice to about 600 men and women in their own homes.

Each of the English language schemes that NEC set up or for which it shared responsibility evolved in its own way, a diversity that merits research and study. Through this evolution and through its co-operation with other organisations, especially those of the ethnic minorities, through its early sponsoring and production of ESL resources, NEC became a centre of collective expertise.

As the years sped by, the teaching of English-as-a-second-language-to-adults progressively shed its 'pin-money', almost amateur, image, and it has now rightly attained the status of a recognised educational discipline with proper professional standards and required qualifications, training courses, text-books and cassettes, learning'teaching packs, TV programmes and its own nation-wide association, NATESLA. To all this NEC made valuable and acknowledged contributions.

From the very beginning and at all times a main purpose for NEC has been the promotion of good inter-community understanding and of reciprocal enrichment through an awareness and an appreciation of different cultures, traditions and outlook.

Placing on record the recollected experiences of just a handful

* Barnet, Brent, Camden, Westminster, Hackney, Haringey, Enfield, Harrow, Hillingdon and Islington.

of the people who worked with NEC – students, teachers, organisers, administrators – this account reflects the excitement of sharing in a project that constantly renewed itself by experimentation, always keen to respond to newly-emergent needs. It shows, we believe, what can be done by a voluntary, independent organisation determined to find ways around the obstacles presented by bureaucracy's rules and regulations.

The experiments and achievements of NEC, the esteem which it attracted both nationally and internationally, are a tribute – and will always remain one – to Ruth Hayman, a founder of NEC, who persuaded, cajoled, encouraged, bullied, challenged and inspired everyone who worked with her. She died in October 1981.

We still miss a unique colleague and beloved friend.

NEIGHBOURHOOD
ENGLISH CLASSES

ORGANISERS
KATHERINE HALLGARTEN
6 BOSCASTLE ROAD
LONDON NW5 1EG
PHONE 01-485-3784

RUTH HAYMAN
GARDEN FLAT
14 LAWN ROAD
LONDON NW3 2XS
01-722-0254

18th May 1971

Mr. Hugh Tinker
Director,
Institute of Race Relations
36 Jermyn Street
London S.W.1.

Dear Mr. Tinker,

This is a request to the City Parochial Foundation from Neighbourhood English Classes for a grant.

N.E.C. was formed early in 1970 to organise classes to teach English to non-English speaking adult newcomers to this country, more especially women. Over the past 15 months N.E.C. has organised 16 classes in the London Boroughs of Brent, Barnet, Camden, Islington, Southall, Wembley and Westminster.

N.E.C. classes are small and are held in easily accessible places such as clinics, schools, and community rooms. Classes range in size from 3 to 24; average attendance is about 8 students.

All N.E.C. teachers are qualified to teach English as a second language. For the most part their salaries are paid by the Adult Education Institutes or Polytechnics in the area in which classes are held; where this cannot be arranged N.E.C. pays the teachers.

The Community Relations Commission made the original grant aid to initiate the project and gave a further grant to cover administrative expenses for the year ending 31st March 1971. The Camden Committee for Community Relations (under whose auspices N.E.C. operates in Camden) made a small donation and three small donations have been obtained from private sources. We have been advised that the C.R.C. will not be able to make any further grants to N.E.C. because it is limited to aiding new projects in the initial stages.

N.F.C. is developing rapidly and there is a growing demand for N.E.C. classes. During this year we plan to start additional classes in the areas in which we are already operating and to extend our work into new areas in and around London. In so doing we shall continue to work in close association with CRO's, health visitors and with organisations such as Task Force, Cambridge House Language Scheme and V.O.S.A.; and in co-operation with educational authorities.

/....

Mr. Hugh Tinker   18th May 1971

This means that the salaries of those of our teachers who are approved by the Principal of the F.E. Institute/Polytechnic concerned will be borne by the local education authority which will also pay the rental of premises for classes where necessary.

There remains the problem of finding administrative expenses including the remuneration of the organisers who have an increasing volume of work to handle. Provision must also be made for teaching materials and aids and to pay those teachers whose salaries are not met by the local authority.

We would be most grateful if you would treat this letter as a formal application to the City Parochial Foundation for a grant of £1,200 a year for three years from 1st January 1972, as a contibution towards our estimated expenses which are set out in the attached Budget.

I hope this application will receive your sympathetic and favourable consideration.

With best wishes,

Yours sincerely,

Ruth Hayman
Organiser N.E.C.

How we began

Katherine Hallgarten with Ruth Hayman

Neighbourhood English Classes began for me in September 1969 when a thin, sunburnt woman walked into my back garden, shook my hand and said,

'Hullo, I'm Ruth Hayman. Let's talk about English classes for immigrant women.'

We talked about the class I was teaching at the Kentish Town Clinic, sponsored by the Camden Committee for Community Relations. We talked for hours about the problems of women, of immigrant women, of illiterate women, of mothers with small children, of trying to learn English in a class full of European au pairs. We talked about black women in South Africa, about Jewish women in London in the 1890s. We talked about colonialism, oppression, racism (racialism it was then called), the role of women in welcoming – or closing the family off from – integration. We talked all afternoon until we ended up with NEIGHBOURHOOD ENGLISH CLASSES – an idea and (because it was Ruth) a programme of action. To start tomorrow.

I would like to allow Ruth to speak for herself about the early days of NEC. Her account is taken from a talk she gave at the International House Teachers Club in January 1972.

NEC was conceived at the bedside of Robert Swann of International House – in a hospital in Maida Vale in 1969. Robert and I have been friends from the time he worked at Amnesty International. I was visiting a very sick Robert and he was telling me about his work in International House in Bangkok. I suddenly said to him, 'What about the immigrants coming into this country? Who is helping them to learn English?' I'd seen women floundering in the shops, looking lost and desolate on street corners, unable to find their way and unable to ask for help. I'd heard of their communication difficulties in hospitals and clinics.

Robert and I decided that for a start I should do a short

teacher-training course to get some idea about language-teaching techniques – I was a lawyer from South Africa and this was a venture into a totally new world. And so I did a two-weeks concentrated course at International House and found it stimulating, exciting and utterly exhausting. I emerged worn-out and limp but with some conception of what language teaching was all about.

My next step was to make enquiries in the Borough of Camden, where I lived, about English language classes, and the first person to whom I was referred was Katherine Hallgarten. Katherine at that time was teaching a class of immigrant women in the Family Welfare Clinic in Kentish Town – we met, and we have worked together ever since then.

Together Katherine and I hammered out the basic elements of NEC (including its name):

1. This was not to be a charity but a professional service. Teaching must be done by qualified teachers who were paid for their work. Students must pay fees – even if only a nominal amount.
2. Classes must be small, informal, and at a familiar place in the neighbourhood, such as the clinic or the school; they must also be easily accessible – that is, students should not have more than an eight- to ten-minutes' walk between home and class.
3. The women seemed to be the most neglected section of the newcomer communities; men learned English at work, children at school, but housebound women were apparently not being reached – so we would cater especially for women.
4. We would teach everyday functional English to enable the women to make use of the amenities available in their neighbourhoods and to give them the means of relating to day-to-day life in this country.

Pilot project

We planned a three-months' pilot project to test out our ideas. In this three months we proposed to start a network of classes in two neighbourhoods – one to be selected in the Borough of Camden and the other in Southall. We approached the Community Relations Commission for a grant to finance this experiment, and the CCCR, the Ealing Community Relations Officer and the

8

Indian Workers' Association in Southall for their co-operation.

The grant came through in January 1970 and we were ready to go.

It soon became clear that three months were quite inadequate to test the potential of the project and that we had seriously underestimated the time and effort required to launch each class. But it was equally clear that there was a need for classes of the type envisaged by NEC. There was already provision for language teaching in classes run by the adult education institutes and, at the other end of the scale, by voluntary language schemes on a one-to-one basis such as that run by Cambridge House and by Margaret Hinchcliffe in Wandsworth. NEC classes could fill the gap between these two.

Accordingly we applied to the Community Relations Commission for further grant-aid to enable us to carry on, and we received support from this source up to the end of March 1971.

Our progress in starting up classes during 1970 was painfully arduous and slow, and by the end of that year we had misgivings because we appeared to have so little to show for all our very hard work. However, in 1971 the picture changed radically and by the end of that year NEC had organised 26 classes in seven London boroughs and had 30 teachers involved in its work.

Administration and finance

Since April 1970 NEC has been managed by an executive committee of nine members, seven of whom are teachers of English as a second language.

We have applied for registration as a charity. Meanwhile we are financed by a three-year grant through the Institute of Race Relations, and by donations from private sources. These include a donation made by Louis Alexander of all the Indian royalties from his English-language textbook, *First Things First*.

Relations with other bodies

At every stage NEC has had good working relations with the Community Relations Commission and with local community relations officers and councils. We also work in co-operation with organisations such as Cambridge House, Volunteers Overseas

Service Association, local health departments and others.

Our relations with education authorities have been more varied. In the areas under the jurisdiction of the Inner London Education Authority, it has been left to the individual principals of adult education institutes to determine their relations with us. With one exception, these principals have taken the NEC classes in their areas under their wing – the NEC teacher is paid through the institute and in some instances premises have been provided and teaching aids supplied. In the borough of Brent, NEC operates directly under the local authority which pays our teachers and provides classrooms on school premises.

NEC students pay the stipulated fees to the adult education authority concerned.

Recruiting of students

The hardest work is recruiting students for the classes and ensuring their continued attendance. Hours and hours in the evenings and over weekends are spent in visiting the homes of potential students, talking to them about the classes, overcoming the natural shyness and timidity of the women, and persuading their husbands to permit them to attend classes. We usually arrange to fetch new students by car to attend class for the first time, which makes it less of an ordeal. Even after students have enrolled it is necessary to keep in touch with them by calling at their homes from time to time, and particularly to do so if a student has been absent from class for a week or so. It is also necessary to call on our students before the start of each term to remind them about the class, and to approach new students before the term begins.

How we start new classes

We either select an area in which a large number of newcomers are living and there appears to be a need for NEC classes, or – and this has happened in recent months – an interested person or organisation approaches us to start a class in a particular area – usually this is coupled with an offer to help us to get the class going.

Local clinics, schools, immigrant organisations, religious institutions and community relations officers are then visited, to ask for their support and to obtain the names and addresses of residents in the area who do not appear to speak English. We consider that 25 to 30 names is the absolute minimum on which to make a start.

The next move is to find suitable premises – a family welfare clinic, or a school – and to make the necessary arrangements with the local community relations officer and with the principal of the local adult education institute, and to find a teacher.

The house-to-house visiting is then done. We use a multi-lingual leaflet which gives information about the classes. If we can get the requisite number of students, the class opens.

Indu Sheth and Jaya Chouhan joined our ranks in 1971 and are now members of our executive committee. They have taken over the recruiting of students in Brent, and the biggest increase in the number of classes has been in this borough. Indu and Jaya maintain regular contact with the students, which has resulted in an exceptionally good attendance record at the classes.

Teachers

NEC teachers are required to be qualified to teach English as a second language. A number of them are also graduates. Several teach during the day at one of the language schools. So far we have not had any difficulty in finding teachers but occasionally there is some delay in matching a teacher to a class.

The teachers are dedicated people, often working under trying circumstances. They are also called upon to do extra unpaid work such as house-to-house visiting of students.

Students

In about ten classes the majority of students are Indian women, mainly Gujerati from East Africa. Those in the class in Southall are Punjabi or Bengali. The two classes in Soho have Chinese men and women students. Six classes have women of several nationalities – Pakistani, Indian, Cypriot, Italian. Two other classes have men and women of several nationalities.

The day classes are attended by mothers who often come accompanied by their pre-school children. Although crêche or other facilities are provided to cope with these babes, they are usually very much in attendance – underfoot, on the chairs or tables, being fed, changed, taken to the loo, scolded and what have you. Lessons are conducted over, above, in spite of and sometimes with the unconscious collaboration of these offspring. The first two classes started by NEC were day classes, but the pattern is changing. It seems that, wherever possible, the women must go to work to supplement the family income. Consequently most of the NEC classes are now held in the evenings and the demand is for more evening classes.

The women students work all day, shop on the way home, and prepare the evening meal for their families before they attend their class. Afterwards they must go home and complete their domestic chores. For this reason they have asked that the evening class be limited to one hour and a quarter per session. All NEC classes meet twice a week.

The numbers in a class vary from about five to 17. Some of the adult education principals insist on a minimum enrolment of 12 or 13. This can lead to much hurrying and scurrying at the start of a term. In one instance recently the NEC had to carry a student from her sick bed to enrol, and two others who were absent because of Ramadan were persuaded to come along just to enrol. They then returned home to their observances.

Syllabus and material

NEC has devised its own syllabus which is revised periodically. It is geared to everyday situations – at the clinic, emergency phone calls, street directions, having a broken utensil fixed ... With the advent of male students, the teachers concerned with teaching them have devised dialogues for attending football matches, watching telly, and so on.

Our aim is to help newcomers to participate in everyday life in this country, not to coach them to reach O-level English. Accordingly, our primary task is to give the students the confidence to speak and to speak so that they can be understood, even if they can't pronounce all their consonants correctly, or continue to have a marked accent. The measure of attainment is, for example, when a student has sufficient confidence and linguistic skill to visit the doctor alone and not, as hitherto, accompanied by son or husband as protector and interpreter.

This year we plan to extend our material to include more complex situations and relationships such as a tenant in relation to his landlord, a wage earner wanting a rise, hire-purchase agreements, and so on.

Standards

The standards of the students vary considerably as do their individual abilities to learn. Some are illiterate in their own language and have never experienced the discipline of a classroom. Others can read and write English but cannot speak it and have a limited comprehension. Ages range from late teens to middle age or elderly.

This wide range of standards inevitably leads to difficulties for the teacher, and one way in which we try to help is by arranging for an unqualified volunteer assistant to attend the class. The teacher can then divide the class into groups for separate activities for part of the time, with the volunteer taking charge of one group and the teacher the other.

Methods of teaching

The students are warm and friendly, and once they have got over their initial shyness they are very responsive. For many of the women these classes are their only social contact outside their families and are treated therefore as a social occasion. One new student said recently, 'Three months ago I had no friends. Today you are all my friends.'

Teachers use the usual techniques and aids (except the expensive ones such as tape recorders), but work proceeds at a much slower pace than in a class at a language school or in an adult education institute.

In addition, teachers arrange expeditions or projects: a cooking session, a walk in the street to practise street directions, a shopping expedition to compare prices in the local shops ...

Games such as Hunt the Thimble and O'Grady Says – suitably modified – are used; also some educational games such as word lotto. We also find that from a very early stage the students want to read and write, and demand books and homework, both for use and to show that they are going to school.

As there is a dearth of reading and writing materials we have tried our hand at producing some worksheets, and although these are rather crude and amateurish they have been well received and we are now in the course of preparing another batch.

Ruth's passionate enthusiasm, energy, clear analysis of need and fanatical attention to detail comes through in this talk, just as it permeated all aspects of her private and working life.

Indeed there was little distinction for Ruth and her friends between the two. We all became her friends; we all turned to her for valued personal advice. 'Hi, Katherine,' she would greet me. 'I'll take the children into the kitchen for a drink – you go and have a whisky with Merv – you both look shattered.' Ruth's husband, Mervyn, and their children, Peter, Janet, Stephen and Alan, were always up to date on the latest NEC achievement or catastrophe and always wanted to hear the most recent gossip over a drink or a meal.

Ruth's encouragement and enthusiasm gave many of us in the field of English as a Second Language a start in a permanent career. For all of us her vitality and her Aquarian instinct that the world must be kicked into better shape was an inspiration for which we are grateful.

Postscript – January 1984

Last week we went canvassing for prospective students in the Archway area, in the northernmost reaches of Islington's Adult Education Institute. There were four of us: three full-time ESL workers and one part-time ESL tutor, all of us paid by the local education authority. As we tramped round the streets in the pouring rain taking leaflets into shops, launderettes and community centres, talking to head teachers, social workers and health visitors, I remembered similar visits in Kings Cross, the Portobello Road, Gerrard Street, Homerton Road – through whole areas of central and outer London, stretching back into the early years of NEC.

Today, as Islington's Adult Education Institute's ESL organiser, I have a staff of two full-time workers and 30 part-time tutors. We have access to resources officers who help us to make videos and tapes and to write publicity material. We have a borough language co-ordinator to draw together and extend ESL provision for everyone over 16, and a part-time Home Tutor Organiser, Frances Weinreich, who works with 60 pairs of students and volunteers.

I am now part of an ESL provision in the Inner London Education Area. More than 12,000 students are learning ESL in our adult education institutes or colleges of further education. Again and again, as I attend meetings, I meet people familiar to

14

me from early NEC days, teachers who began as volunteers, and whose first introduction to ESL was in Ruth's flat in Lawn Road.

English as a second language has developed into an integral part of adult and further education. Methods, ideas and new ways have grown from the early days when Ruth, in north London, and Margaret Hinchliffe in Wandsworth, first inspired groups of volunteers to walk round the streets in the pouring rain, canvassing for prospective students.

We have come a long way.

The Secretary
Voluntary Workers' Bureau
Camden Council of Social Service
25 Euston Road
London NW1

Camden Council of Social Service 722 - 0794   VOLUNTARY
WORKERS'
BUREAU

Date 19 - 11 -   19 7 0

To MRS R. Hayman
Garden Flat. 14, Lawn Road NW 3

This is to introduce *Mr/Mrs/Miss Frances Weinreich

of 49 Brookfield, 5, Highgate West Hill

who is interested in being considered for voluntary work with your

organization as a helper — N.E. Classes.
r Teacher

Will you kindly detach and complete the stamped addressed card below
and return it to me.

? Raglan Street clinic   R. S. Hubback
                                   Secretary

Early days

Joyce Thomas

I was lucky enough to be in at the inception of NEC, and to watch its development over the years.

At the end of 1969, when Ruth and Katherine were planning to set up their first classes, I was a home tutor in the one-to-one English language teaching organisation run by Katherine in Camden. At that time (before it became a part of NEC), it was run in collaboration with the Cambridge House Language Scheme in Camberwell and the Camden Committee for Community Relations.

Home tutors had no training apart from periodical one-day seminars and some instructional hand-outs.

I soon realised that even for informal sessions in the home, some training would be invaluable. Katherine recalled that I had consulted her about this, and suggested that I might like to take an intensive short course in teaching English as a Foreign Language at International House – similar to a course which Ruth had recently taken – with a view to, possibly, teaching in NEC if and when it got off the ground.

I was glad to do this even though I felt some trepidation. I was far from young and had no previous connection with teaching. But the course proved stimulating and enjoyable.

Ruth and Katherine had leaflets printed in various languages, and we started to publicise NEC. Katherine was already running a class in a Kentish Town clinic, and another was opening in Ealing; we intended to start a second one in Kentish Town, some distance from the first.

We all did a great deal of visiting at that time. We handed out leaflets at clinics, doctors' surgeries, libraries, Citizens Advice Bureaux, Asian shops. We visited the local schools, where we found a varied reception. One head teacher, for example, couldn't have been more enthusiastic and helpful; another dismissed us curtly, saying we couldn't expect to make use of the school's organisation for our purposes. We visited the homes of possible students whose addresses had been given to us. We quickly learned that it was essential to do this in the evenings or at the weekends when it was likely that male relatives or older children with some knowledge of English would be at home.

In spite of all this canvassing, students were slow to come forward at first – perhaps because many Asian families had not realised the many occasions on which women would need to understand English, above all when attending clinics. One nursing sister told me of a lady who, with her husband's agreement, had decided to go on the pill. She returned the next day, very distressed, with the empty bottle, having apparently taken all the pills at once. Luckily, all was well. In the course of time she had bouncing twins.

Marjorie Beadle, a professional English-language teacher living in Camden, was asked to prepare the first NEC elementary English course. Our first committee was set up, consisting of Ruth, Katherine, Marjorie and myself.

The planned Camden class opened in March 1970 in a far-from-ideal classroom in the Neighbourhood Advice Centre with no more than five students. I was the teacher, and have to admit it was not a howling success! – although one mother brought her baby who yelled most of the time. She said it was too upsetting for everyone, and gave up. Another young woman departed to take up a job – and so it went on. So that when the Advice Centre left the premises because they were due to be pulled down, we too decided to close, intending to re-open in better premises in the autumn.

I learned the necessity of accepting the fact that students would often be absent: illness, bad weather and family occasions were among the causes. I realised also how excellent it would be if we could have someone to look after the infants brought along by our students.

All the initial work done by the founders was beginning to bear fruit. NEC was becoming well known and making many friends. Indu Sheth joined the committee and did very valuable work in Brent. Many more classes opened. The principal of Marylebone Institute was very sympathetic to our work and sponsored classes in that area. We started an evening class in West Hampstead, which I taught in its early stages, and discovered that mixed classes *were* viable – we had been warned that they were not. Two delightful Indian air hostesses, Mala Dhondi and Usha Frami, came and helped us with our home visiting and became involved in that first evening class.

In the summer of 1971 I took over the organising of Camden home tutors. It was interesting to see how classes and home tutoring complemented one another. In most cases, classes were desirable, but inevitably there were some people who could not get out and needed tuition at home.

In 1972 the Ugandan Asians arrived. By then NEC was well-equipped to arrange English language teaching for them and for the later mass arrivals who needed help. It had expanded in those first two or three years in what I think now was an almost incredible way – entirely justifying Ruth's belief in the need. Her imaginative approach to new propositions put to NEC was occasionally daunting to some of us, but she always succeeded in meeting requests, and she was always ready to experiment with new ideas.

We never stood still, and it was her unbounded energy that guaranteed NEC's success.

Telling the time and catching a train

This lesson plan, outlined by an NEC classroom teacher, was prompted by the needs of her students to understand first, how to tell the time and next, how to make use of their knowledge. They had also to be taught how to ask for time-related information. Many of these elements were drawn together here, demonstrating the Western obsession with time and time-connected activities. The class was mixed-level and held in an inner-city clinic; one has to imagine the teaching taking place against a background of children playing noisily under the care of the Child Helper.

A Lesson Plan

Telling the time and catching a train

Procedure	Aids
i) <u>Revision</u> : telling the time	cardboard clock face
ii) <u>New work</u> : railway station vocabulary :	

ticket office	passengers
clerk	platform
single fare	barrier
return fare	porter
half fare	arrivals
timetable	departures

Elicit as many of these words as possible from the students.

Susan lives in Birmingham. Mary lives in London. Susan is going to visit Mary in London. At 10 o'clock the train leaves for London. At 12 o'clock it arrives in London.	picture of Susan picture of Mary

iii) <u>check</u> : When does the train leave ?
　　　　　　What time does it arrive ?

iv) <u>drill</u> : It takes 2 hours.
　　　　　　It takes 1½ hours ... etc.

v) <u>dialogue</u> : Susan : When is the next train to
　　　　　　　　　London, please ?
　　　　　Clerk : At 10.
　　　　　Susan : How long does it take ?
　　　　　Clerk : 2 hours.

Drill students in pairs, using simple timetable on blackboard :

Departure from Birmingham	Arrival in London
8.00 a.m.	10.00 a.m.
9.30	11.30
10.00	12.00 noon/p.m.

Advanced students proceed to real timetable.	railway timetable

Penny Phillips 1984

How long does it take?

Time of departure   Time of arrival

It takes 2 hours.

It takes 3 hours.

It _ _ _ _ _ _ _ _ _ _ _ _.

_ _ _ _ _ _ _ _ _ _ _ _ _ _.

_ _ _ _ _ _ _ 4 _ _ _ _ _ _.

WHEN?

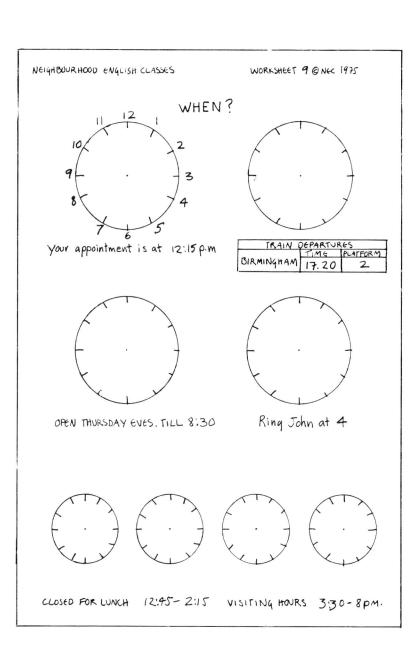

Your appointment is at 12:15 p.m.

TRAIN DEPARTURES		
	TIME	PLATFORM
BIRMINGHAM	17.20	2

OPEN THURSDAY EVES. TILL 8:30   Ring John at 4

CLOSED FOR LUNCH   12:45 – 2:15   VISITING HOURS   3:30 – 8 p.m.

Who were the teachers?

Betty Jacobs

To be a teacher in NEC in its heyday was exciting, fun, exhausting, challenging. It was to be not only a teacher but a social worker and a friend. It was to be part of a pioneering movement whose aim was to spread knowledge of English in the immigrant (new settler) community. In the two-way process, the cause of racial harmony was helped and there was immeasurable enrichment for teachers and students in the exchange of knowledge about different cultures.

Teachers came into NEC from a variety of backgrounds. Many were school teachers; some taught at language schools; a number were graduates. Often they were housewives and mothers who could not take full-time jobs. But they had to be qualified to teach English as a Second Language by modern methods.

Those who were keen but not qualified took a training course at International House, the teacher training institute in London (then in Shaftesbury Avenue, now in Piccadilly). Some gained a little experience as classroom volunteers, before or afterwards. Some, like myself, went straight into the course and landed jobs with NEC afterwards.

It was an inch-long paragraph in a newspaper which led me indirectly to Ruth Hayman and a new career. I was at that time a journalist, writing for New Zealand newspapers about life in England, but I'd lived away from my country for a long time and wanted a change. The newspaper item stated that many immigrant children were at a disadvantage when they started school because they didn't know English nursery rhymes and stories. That would be an enjoyable and worth-while thing to do, to teach them, I thought. But how to reach those who were not attending nursery schools and play groups? I made enquiries and was eventually advised to contact Ruth.

I ended up teaching not children – but their mothers. And I found it a stimulating new field of endeavour which in many ways changed my life. I formed warm and friendly relationships with students which have in some instances lasted for years, and I felt I learnt as much from them as they did from me.

When I began to teach my first class in Wembley on April 20, 1971, NEC had been in existence for only a year. Yet by the end of 1971 there were 26 classes with 30 teachers in seven London boroughs.

There was no typical NEC teacher. We were of all ages, we came from different backgrounds, we even spoke English with different accents since some of us came from other countries. We might turn up in class wearing a maxi dress, trouser suit, or cardie and tweed skirt. Our students were sometimes surprised by our informal way of teaching, having been used to a more disciplined type of education in their own lands.

One quality we probably all shared was a desire to serve the community in some way. Not that we thought of ourselves as do-gooders – and Ruth and Katherine were adamant that we were not. From the beginning they were determined that NEC should offer a professional service. Qualified teachers would be used and be paid for their work. Students must pay fees, however nominal.

NEC always attracted more women teachers than men. This was partly because of the difficulty of making a full-time living out of ESL teaching, and partly because in areas with a high proportion of women students, female teachers were preferred. However there was never any question of women entirely running the show. Men were always welcomed.

Ruth's enthusiasm warmed me, and her encouragement was something for which I shall always be grateful. It was, after all, a gamble for me. I had no idea whether I would prove a good teacher or not. Indeed, in the first couple of years, when Ruth was skilfully winkling funds out of important bodies, it was alarming to have her descend on a class with visitors (though always with advance warning). Nerve-wracking to feel that upon one's classroom 'demonstration' depended the success or failure of her appeal for money!

Sometimes a VIP from International House came to observe, but if Ruth or the visitor had any criticism or advice to offer, it always came privately, afterwards. In later years, when as experienced teachers some of us were asked to observe new teachers and to put in reports as to their suitability, we were able to temper any criticism with kindness, having been through it ourselves.

Sympathy has always been an important element in the NEC

NOTES FOR NEW TEACHERS

1. **WELCOME**

   In terms of the NEC Constitution, once you are conducting a class run/
   organised by NEC, you automatically become a member of the NEC Organisation and are entitled to attend Annual and Special General Meetings
   and to have a say in the policy and conduct of the Organisation.

2. **APPOINTMENT**

   We have recommended your appointment to the ....
   Authority / Department / Institute / College.

   A representative of NEC will visit your class, probably within the
   first six weeks of your employment, to assess the position and report
   to the authority on the progress being made.

   As your class/group is a new one/experimental venture, it will be
   necessary to keep a close watch on it, and if it is not viable, the
   Authority / Department / Institute / College (or NEC itself) may
   decide to close it and to terminate your services.

3. **PROCEDURE RE REGISTER, RECEIPT BOOK AND STUDENTS' FEES**

   (a) I enclose a note about the procedure in Brent

   (b) Please contact ....to obtain all details

   (c) The representative of the Authority / Department / Institute /
       College responsible for overseeing your class is

       .... Please be in
       touch with her/him about this and other class formalities

4. **KIT, MATERIALS, TAPE RECORDER**

   I enclose a list of the contents of the NEC Teachers' Kit. Your Kit,
   and other NEC material, is available and can be collected from our
   office between 9.30 a.m. and 5.15 p.m. on weekdays. A deposit of
   £2.50 is payable on the Kit. Please phone to make an appointment.

   If you need a cassette recorder for use in your class, please contact the NEC office.

   Books - NEC has a useful reference library, a small loan library
   including sets of easy readers, and supplies of Senior Scope books
   for sale. Alternatively, Scope and other books can be ordered
   through your local bookshop or through the LCL Bookshop, 126 Camden
   Road, London NW1 (485 6465)

5. MIXED ABILITY CLASS - VOLUNTEER ASSISTANT(S)

Most NEC classes are ungraded and teachers find it helpful to have the assistance of a volunteer. Our volunteers attend one session a week. If you find that you could use the services of a volunteer, please contact

....

6. CHILD HELPER

We employ child helpers to care for pre-school children accompanying their mothers to class. If you need a child helper, please contact Annie Millet either via the office or at home:

8 Ockenden Road, London N1 (359 2229)

7. RELIEF PANEL

We have a panel of relief teachers and can supply you with the names of some whom you could approach in the event of your not being able to take your class. We hope that you will join this panel.

8. OUTSIDE THE CLASSROOM

(a) The active recruitment of students is a very important aspect of NEC's work and we look to the teachers to help by home-visiting potential students referred to them and by following up students who have stopped coming to class. The local home tutor organiser / language scheme co-ordinator is

....
and she will be in touch with you about this and other matters.

(b) Class outings, visits to your class by outside speakers or visitors for a special function give your students extra language practice and a chance to relate to the community. For suggestions / ideas please contact Elaine Self (458 1046)

(c) Teachers are expected to attend termly seminars run by NEC which are invaluable for keeping teachers in touch with the Executive Committee and with developments in teaching techniques and materials.

9. PUBLIC STATEMENTS

As a member of NEC you should not make any statement or issue any publicity material on behalf of the Organisation without the prior approval of a member of the NEC Executive Committee

10. PRIVATE TEACHING

It is NEC policy that no NEC teacher should give private lessons to NEC students. If NEC students want to arrange extra paid private tuition, they should obtain a teacher through a commercial organisation, and not through the NEC network.

'teacher's kit'. Many of us had come from other countries ourselves or had worked abroad and understood the problems of new settlers. For some, English was not their mother tongue – and there are today more of these teachers among the younger people than there used to be – so they too brought special understanding.

NEC's high standards were adhered to even when circumstances were trying – inadequate premises and materials (teachers had mostly to make their own) and the presence of toddlers and babies in class, though crêches were sometimes available. Teachers' and students' voices had to rise above the noise; rôle-playing went on with small children under-foot. The important thing was that the mothers should be there!

NEC teachers were also required to do house-to-house visiting, either to recruit new students, give a reminder about the start of a new term, or enquire why a student had been absent.

From the earliest days teachers involved themselves in organising coach trips to well-known places in order to widen their students' knowledge of this country. The sharing of picnic lunches sitting on the grass at stately homes or at the seaside was enjoyable for everyone.

Fund-raising, too, was tackled as a class project – either for NEC's own funds or for selected charities, giving our students the feeling of belonging to the wider community and of having something to contribute to it.

This sense of the teacher being a link with the world outside has always been strong in NEC. Often the teacher has been the student's only contact with English-speaking people on a social level. The class itself was also important because it gave the students the chance to speak English to one another – although sometimes the teacher had to threaten to fine those who chattered in their own language during a lesson!

'But do you have to be able to speak the students' languages?' is a question frequently asked of ESL teachers. Of course the answer is no, we teach by direct method. This is the method used at International House where English as a Foreign Language (EFL) is taught, appropriate to those who come to England to study and will then return home. It had to be adapted to the needs of the new settlers. Thus, a few years ago, the term English as a Second Language (ESL) came to be used and teacher-training courses specifically in this subject were developed and are now held in various parts of the country.

NEC teachers usually had to cope with different levels of

ability within one class, and group work was therefore necessary. Sometimes volunteer assistants were available but teachers still had to prepare what the volunteers were to do. Preparation could take as much time as the actual teaching. There was a time when I had two volunteers in a class with four levels of ability. My time-table was split up into 15-minute sessions, with all of us occupied over the two hours and myself spinning around to each group in turn. Breathless, happy days!

NEC teachers also coped with having students from different countries in the same class. Usually there were others from the same country who could help the beginners a little with translation. At other times there would be a solitary learner, knowing no English, completely out on a limb. Somehow the teacher and student had to crawl along that branch towards each other and to find some point of contact.

At NEC seminars over the years, teachers found warmth and stimulation – meeting colleagues, gaining help with problems and sharing new ideas.

For racial harmony, bridges have to be built between the host community and the newcomers. Teachers and students in NEC classes have together played a significant part in this bridge-building.

Beginners – pioneers all

Nora Gutmann

One not so fine day in 1971, after having worked for 12 years as a translator of newsfilm commentary for the BBC, I was declared redundant.

I could not fight against the redundancy of my job, but I was not going to accept redundancy of myself. I searched for signposts to useful employment and found one which said: 'Neighbourhood English Classes'. Teaching English was not completely related to what I had been doing – but what appealed to me most was the 'neighbourhood' aspect. It implied community work and seemed the most promising antidote against being made superfluous.

When I found out more, I realised that my new 'neighbours' would be mostly dark-skinned exiles from Uganda, who had begun to appear in many High Streets that year, Marks and Spencer cardigans over their delicate, graceful saris the only concession to English fashion and English climate. I was apprehensive. How could I ever bridge the gap between my world and theirs – they seemed so distant and remote.

But there was also the realisation that I had come, as it were, full circle: 35 years ago I had to escape from persecution in my country and had found asylum in England. Surely this common experience would be a bond between us and would help me to help them.

I was invited to sit in on a class in Park Lane, Wembley, which had been established the previous year. About 15 Asian women of varying ages, from slim young girls to matronly grandmothers, were crowded into a tiny room, filling the air with the fragrant scent of incense stick and curry, as well as with occasional bursts of Gujerati chatter.

What struck me most at that first meeting was the mixture of sisterly familiarity and respectful deference towards their teacher, the warmth and outgoing friendliness which immediately removed all imaginary barriers and doubts, and the

30

unhurried poise of their bearing. These first impressions have prevailed through many years of teaching. Even apologetic late-comers to class always approach with the same slow, measured step and I have long since given up trying to hurry students to catch a bus or hurry them to keep an appointment, for they will not submit to the tyranny of time.

The next practical step for me was to take an intensive course at International House to learn the techniques for teaching English by direct method to multi-lingual classes.

Fortified with a diploma and an armory of new and exciting teaching ideas and methods, I presented myself six weeks later to Ruth Hayman, whose name had already become a beacon for aspiring student-teachers. The interview was conducted in Ruth's typical kind and matter-of-fact way in her flat which at that time served also as her office.

I emerged, reassured by her sympathetic encouragement, impressed by her high professional standards and efficiency, infected by her enthusiasm and a little overawed by her passion for new challenges and commitments. This passion would sometimes prove uncomfortable for those of us who were content to leave well alone – an attitude which was anathema to her.

I was accepted as a prospective teacher but before being given a class of my own was advised to sit in for a month or two at as many NEC classes as possible. I served this most valuable apprenticeship in, amongst others, Betty Jacobs' classes in Wembley and Shirin Spencer's classes in Kilburn.

My first assignment was an evening class in Gladstone Park Junior School, NW10. Then followed three day-time classes in Wembley, Sudbury and Kensal Green.

I very soon realised that I had to make a significant change from teaching English as a foreign language to teaching English as a second language. Our students, who at that time were mostly non-English-speaking Asian adults with a sprinkling of other nationalities, didn't need diplomas and certificates, but the very basic linguistic tools for every-day living in a new environment. They needed the language skills to cope with manifold situations, from shopping at a time when Asian supermarkets and pharmacies had not yet replaced the English corner shop and the English chemist, to being able to respond to an English neighbour's attempts to establish a friendly relationship.

This desperate need to overcome the painfully isolating communication barrier on all levels produced the sense of urgency and of meaningful endeavour which was so characteristic of the classroom atmosphere during those first years of NEC work.

There existed also a spirit of pioneering which was emphasised by the often makeshift nature of our meeting places, in corners of vast, draughty church halls or in small, cluttered store rooms.

Pioneering had to be done in many areas, and Ruth Hayman, the arch-pioneer, involved her teachers actively in many of her stratagems for NEC.

When more accommodation was required for the ever-growing number of classes, we were sent to explore our areas for hospitable churches, community centres, clinics, etc., where we could obtain rooms for day classes at a nominal charge. In Brent, churches of various denominations were most sympathetic to our cause and have, over the years, been very helpful and supportive.

My four classes represented some of the varying social, cultural and educational backgrounds of our students at that time. There were the comparatively well-established gentle matriarchs of Sudbury and Wembley. They had known an urban life and had enjoyed educational advantages. Although deeply rooted in their own religious and cultural traditions, they were receptive and open to new ideas and experiences. After the first foundations were laid, these women often moved on to more sophisticated subjects and vocabulary.

There were the grandmothers and the young mothers with numerous babies and toddlers, of the Mortimer Road Child Care Clinic. They often came from small villages in India, had little or no formal education and were frequently illiterate in their own languages. They usually appeared to be bewildered and lost at the beginning, but soon they grew into extremely jolly, lively class-families, with language requirements and capacities remaining at a very basic level.

Luckily Ann Hettich soon arrived on the scene as full-time Language Scheme Organiser for Brent. She eased the cheerful but sometimes chaotic conditions in the clinic class by arranging for child helpers, who sometimes succeeded in enticing the children away from their mothers and involving them in games and creative activities. Encouraging the mothers to play with their children in the way the helpers did was not always so successful, for traditions with regard to this aspect of child care were very different.

And then there were the young men and women who, after a work-day which for the women usually started at five a.m., came

PAST AND PRESENT STORIES

Extracts from the booklet written and illustrated by students and teacher of an NEC class in Harlesden, North London, and issued in May 1978.

Introduction

We are a class of men and women. Some of us are married, and some of us are unmarried. Some of us are working, and some of us are students, and some are unemployed. Three of us work in a factory. One works in a shop, one in a conference centre, one on a building site, and one in a restaurant. Seven of us are from India, one from Spain, one from Pakistan, one from Tanzania, and one from Turkey. We have been in England for between 6 months and 6 years. We have come to evening classes at the Furness Road school to learn English, because we need to speak with English people at work, or when we go shopping, and to write letters. It's a good class because we've got a good teacher and she asks us if we remember or not. We decided to write stories for this magazine. We decided to tell Jane (our teacher) to correct our stories because if we made a lot of mistakes people wouldn't understand. Thank you for reading our stories. We hope you like them.

What did I do last week?

At 7.30 each morning I got up. I had a bath and my breakfast. I got dressed. At 9.00 a.m. I went to the school with my children. Then I went to work. At 3.00 p.m. I had my lunch. At 11.00 p.m. I finished with my work. All day I work very hard and I serve more than a hundred people a day. I started at 10 a.m. in the morning and finished at 11.00 pm at night in the restaurant. I am off only one day. If I did not work these hours,

I cannot get enough money for my family. I must work long hours. When I am off I go to see my friend some time. But all the time I'm worried about my family in my country, Turkey.

Hüseyin Düzgün.

This story is about English

When I came from India I didn't know how to speak but in one month there was a letter. It said that they have found the school so I went to school with my father and then I spoke a little bit of English, then I had lots of friends. Then I went to another school and that time I went off alone. After four years I spoke English better than before. So I tried very hard and now I can speak English.

Kanbai Derbhi.

to my evening class in Gladstone Park. The majority of these students were working in factories and therefore had more contact with and experience of the world outside their homes. They were perhaps the most highly motivated learners – a fact that also contributed to their often amazing progress.

However much the classes differed in composition and background, there were at least two factors which were common to all of them: the love and affection the students had, in my experience, for all their teachers, and the strong community feeling within the class, embracing all the nationalities which found their way into NEC.

One of my older Sudbury students, who has managed to remain triumphantly immune to my efforts to modify her bad speaking habits, told me recently: 'My husband he say why you watch Poland news in TV – you not know Poland, but I say him, I am watch Poland because I have Polish friend in English class, I wanting to know about Poland.'

No sooner had we happily settled into a routine of teaching than Ruth urged us to branch out into different areas of involvement with our students. The words 'extra curricular activities' were added to our termly class-report forms. They referred to outings and trips to the English countryside and places of cultural and historical interest. It was felt that the time had come to establish a link between our students and the community, so we arranged for representatives of various social services, health workers, nutrition experts, policemen to come to the classroom and speak about their work. We organised fund-raising parties and bring and buy sales for charitable purposes. The best responses to these activities came from our Wembley and Sudbury classes who, thanks to bring and buy sales of Indian foods and handicrafts, were able to present a handsome donation towards a swimming pool for handicapped children in Brent as well as a hand-embroidered wall-hanging, executed by an English artist, which was installed in Brent Town Hall in an official ceremony. Betty Jacobs' parties in Wembley, with delicious Indian and Japanese food and dance-and-song entertainments, became well known and were always reported in the local press.

There were also projects which failed – presumably because of the erroneous idea that what is good and desirable for English people must also be good and desirable for Asian people. A great deal of planning and effort was invested in establishing an Asian Club in Alperton, where men and women could meet and talk and create their own entertainments. After a grand opening, the club died a slow and quiet death. The autopsy established lack of interest from people whose lives were centred predominantly within the family circle and the home. Times have changed. Now, of course, there is a flourishing Brent Indian Association in Wembley, set up and run by the Asian community itself.

Particularly during the first years, this need to know what was relevant to our students' lives and experiences was one of the most baffling of our tasks. Our course books were little help – at that time they were almost entirely geared to European eating and drinking habits, European pastimes and life-styles. But here again Ruth Hayman, who concerned herself not only with the overall grand strategy of NEC but with every detail of classroom work, came to the rescue, organising a flow of NEC worksheets and NEC lesson plans related to the needs of our students.

In 1970 Ruth created what became for teachers the most important event of every term: the seminars. They were a welcome and very necessary opportunity to meet colleagues and organisers, to exchange experiences and ask advice, to air our views and discuss our problems, and to explore new teaching methods.

There were always stimulating lectures and explorations of new techniques, as well as demonstrations of new teaching aids (the tape recorder for example) and useful workshops.

After two years of coming to my class one of my students said to me: 'Before I started coming to English classes, I never dared to go into my garden when I saw my neighbour in hers. I was scared that she would try to talk to me. But now I always go out when I see her and we talk and she comes to my house to try Indian dishes.'

Perhaps this is what it is all about.

English for special purposes

Frances Weinreich

It is difficult to draw a line between 'ordinary' NEC activities and English for special purposes. Each NEC class is different and we have always sought to take into account the special needs of every group of students – in fact, of every individual student.

Our students have always come from an enormous range of places and backgrounds. The Ugandan Asians who arrived in 1972 were the first refugees to stretch the resources of the still new NEC. The authorities had thought it would not be necessary to make special English language provision for them since the majority would have spoken English in Uganda. I remember Ruth saying, very strongly, how wrong the authorities were. As she realised, a very large number of the men needed English tuition at every level, while most of the women spoke Gujerati as their first language, Swahili as their second, and English quite often as a very poor third.

As a voluntary body we could be flexible and innovatory, and we managed to organise tutors both to teach English and to train volunteers in the resettlement camps. Once the refugees had found accommodation, many in Brent and Harrow, we set up Workseeker courses for them, adapted existing classes and started as many new classes as we could with our very limited funding.

We were also able to help with the first South Vietnamese refugees to arrive in 1976. In co-operation with the British Council for Aid to Refugees (BCAR) we began by running a three-month intensive course. It developed into a nearly continuous programme with successive groups of refugees from Vietnam, Ethiopia and Chile.

BCAR commented: 'This venture has since proved a tremendous success. Not only did the refugees make excellent progress in English but the classes played a valuable role socially in bringing together people of different nationalities, races and backgrounds who learned to understand and help each other.'

The result proved so valuable that BCAR took over the courses and two of the NEC teachers as staff.

A somewhat different service was provided for Chilean students here under the auspices of the World University Service (WUS). They needed an intensive summer course so that they would be able to follow college lectures in the autumn – not the survival-level English more usual in our classes.

Linked classes – English with sewing, for instance – which are now an accepted part of many good local ESL schemes, were tried and developed by NEC. There was a language group bringing together both English and non-English speaking mothers and their toddlers. The English-speaking mothers were given a specially-tailored training course to enable them to help the immigrant mothers.

Outside circumstances sometimes prompted us to launch special projects. Impending elections led to courses on the electoral system. Publicity about the occurrence of rickets among Asian toddlers and adolescents led to health-based material being prepared.

Many of our innovatory projects have been health-oriented. As early as 1971 a course for non-English-speaking nurses was tried – and failed. Perhaps it was a bit too far ahead of its time. In 1973 a very successful on-site course at University College Hospital for domestic and ancillary workers was run in conjunction with Pathway Further Education Centre. Novel features were incorporated. The tutors went into the hospital to assess the potential students at work so that a relevant course could be planned. During the course worksheets were distributed to the students, to their supervisors, to nursing staff and even to patients so that the learners could practise their newly-acquired English straightaway.

In 1976 we ran a more advanced course at St. Mary's Hospital. Here the participants were in charge of domestic workers and were being hampered by their inadequate spoken and written English. This most successful scheme was taken over by the newly-formed local Industrial Language Training Unit. We had discovered that in-service training demanded specialised skills and materials, and we were delighted that a part of our work would now receive the attention it deserved.

In 1976 I was appointed NEC organiser in a small local scheme under the umbrella of the Hanley Road Area Improvement Project in the London borough of Islington, funded by central government. After researching the needs of the community I set up day classes at the project centre and primary school, an evening class and a very small home tutor scheme.

The City of London Maternity Hospital was in the area. A year earlier a friend of mind had had her baby there, sharing a room with three Greek women, none of whom spoke adequate English. Since the project encouraged innovatory work I made immediate contact with the nursing staff. They were well aware that communication problems existed and promoted my idea for a weekly visit to the hospital and for the setting up of an ante-natal English class. Prospective students were referred to me by the ante-natal clinic.

Who would think that a maternity hospital would be the place to teach English? Why not? Locating and motivating women whose daily lives are most handicapped by lack of English has always been a problem.

This hospital work has continued for seven years and is now part of the Islington Institute Language Scheme. I usually see my 'students' only after their confinement. The very co-operative staff greet me with 'I've got two ladies for you in Room 2.' Armed with my multi-lingual leaflets I introduce myself and explain that I can help them to learn English. When appropriate I give a little impromptu lesson to demonstrate that learning English is possible. With an A - Z and up-to-date class-lists for our area and for neighbouring boroughs I am usually able to suggest a nearby class to each woman, after which I pass on details to the local ESL organiser. Recently I have met a number of women having new babies at the hospital who, since their last baby, have been attending English classes or have had a home tutor.

Some expectant mothers are admitted into the hospital as in-patients. Unless there are medical reasons against it I try to teach at their bedside the English so desperately needed for their stay in hospital. I find that normal requests, social vocabulary and the giving of information take priority over strictly medical matters. Some women I've known have dramatically improved their English during an enforced stay in hospital – though I wouldn't suggest this as a universal practice!

Sometimes I am able to help with a communication difficulty in the hospital. For instance, using pictures I was able to explain to a weeping mother that her baby had been taken from her bedside to have treatment for mild jaundice and not for anything more serious. Using only the normal ESL techniques, I could console her where the endeavours of the nursing staff were to no avail.

At this point I became aware of how useful it might be for nursing staff to improve their communication skills. I met Alix Henley, who was then developing her training course for nurses and writing 'The Asian Patient in Hospital and at Home'. She felt that one of the chapters, 'Beating the Language Barrier', needed expansion into a separate topic. Together we worked on the outline of a training course for health workers.

The aim of the course is to help health workers to assess the amount of English that their clients understand and speak, to modify their own language so as to be more easily understood, and to compensate for lack of common language by using supplementary means of communication.

Funding, alas, proved to be particularly difficult. We were keen to run a well-prepared and produced course even at the pilot stage. After a couple of time-consuming and futile applications, we got an enthusiastic reception for the course from the Brent and Harrow Health Education Department. At that stage Alix was too busy to be involved. But since our first pilot course in 1981 I have worked in collaboration with Ann Casey, a health education officer in Brent and Harrow. With the help of other NEC staff, we have run two pilot training courses, one for Brent health visitors and special care baby unit nurses, the second for Harrow health visitors and school nurses.

Since then we have been writing a training manual. Alix looked at our work in its draft form and gave us excellent advice and suggestions. In March 1983, Ann Casey and I addressed the annual conference of health education officers, and lent six pilot copies of the manual for trials. After we have considered the evaluations and – no doubt – made changes, we look forward to its publication. We do, however, miss Ruth's enthusiasm and energy in seeing the project through to its conclusion.

Most of the proven facets of NEC's work are now incorporated into local ESL schemes financed by statutory bodies. Recently the NEC executive agreed to spend its dwindling funds on small innovatory projects in those areas where we still had a direct interest. A toy library was set up in Brent and in Harrow for the use of children of ESL class and home tutor students; home tutor organisers were funded to make a video programme to help train home tutors; and a tape is in preparation as an aid to home tutors.

Though NEC has now handed over most of its responsibilities, we are still breaking new ground, still starting new projects with the enthusiasm that has been the NEC trademark throughout our first thirteen years.

Seminars and materials

Caroline Iffla Romijn

It makes quite good sense for one person to try to record both the seminars NEC held and the materials we produced since they certainly went hand-in-hand. Seminars frequently included presentations of our workshops on teaching materials and sometimes new materials were invented or devised in response to demand. As for the wider community relations purposes of NEC, we relied on seminar discussions far more than on written material to disseminate and develop ideas. In fact, we hesitated to circulate much printed material at all – Ruth always had a healthy scepticism about how many people would bother to read it!

I

But first, our seminars. These were great opportunities for NEC teachers, home tutors and classroom volunteers, staff and executive committee members to meet and swap ideas. Quite apart from the usefulness of the learning sessions, they served a very important social and morale-boosting function for teachers who were mostly working in isolated classes with no regular contact with colleagues.

We were very lucky with the pleasant premises which we were allowed to use – first the North Islington Infant Welfare Centre in Manor Gardens, Islington, and then, later on, the rather larger Gospel Oak Family Health Centre. The administrators of both centres made us welcome and were helpful in every way.

Seminars actually started almost as soon as NEC did. Ruth and Katherine held the first summer school in August 1970. They gave a demonstration of classic ESL situational dialogue teaching, called 'A visit to the Doctor's surgery'. A group of local NEC students came along as guinea pigs and stayed for the second demonstration, when Marjorie Beadle and Joyce Thomas taught with wallcharts.

SEMINAR TOPICS 1976 & 1977

MARCH 1976   SUPPORTING OUR STUDENTS' BACKGROUND CULTURE - Kundry Clarke Head of Department of Community Education, Bethnal Green Adult Education Institute

MY WORK WITH PRE-SCHOOL CHILDREN - Mary Koudis, Organiser in charge of 'SPEAK', Hammersmith Pre-School Language Group

TEACHING INTONATION AND STRESS - Joan Holby, International Teacher Training Institute

JUNE 1976   BOOK INFORMATION SESSION: RECENT BOOKS - Rosemary Reid, Convenor of NEC Course/Materials/Aids Work Party

SURPRISE SESSION: A FOREIGN LANGUAGE READING LESSON - Sandra Nicholls, Lecturer in charge of Teacher Training for RSA Certificate in Teaching English to Adult Immigrants, Westminster College

TEACHERS' POOL SESSION - Object: to feed successful methods into teachers' pool

OCTOBER 1976   WAYS OF USING A TAPE RECORDER - Judith Sansom, English Language Tuition Organiser for Hammersmith

TEACHERS' TALKING TIME - Some NEC teachers' ideas

MARCH 1977   THE SILENT WAY - Demonstration by Numa Markee, International House

NEC FORUM - Questions and Problems

WORKSHOP: PLANNING SESSIONS FOR THE MIXED ABILITY CLASS

JUNE 1977   PLANNING YOUR TEACHING FOR A TERM OR LONGER - Sally Stewart Director, ILEA, (North of the River) Industrial Language Training Unit

PRESENTATION OF NEW ENGLISH LANGUAGE TEACHING MATERIAL - Michael Barker, Evans Brother Ltd

CLASS MANAGEMENT - Observations from Executive Committee

HINTS & TIPS PANEL - Sally Stewart, ILTU; Sandra Nicholls, Westminster College; Eun Johns, Tim Lowe and Pete Cranston, International House.

NOVEMBER 1977   BARRIERS - A showing of the film 'SINGH 171' and discussion led by Jenny Lo, Employment Officer, CCCR

TWO WORKSHOPS ON TEACHING MATERIALS - Tony Riley, Warwick-shire Industrial Language Training Unit; Frances Weinreich, NEC, Hanley Road Project

Later in the day there were discussions on the use of games, on blackboard drawing, on the first NEC course and on reading and writing. 'Some discussion took place,' according to the report, 'about the difficulties of teaching students who are illiterate in their own language.' For many of us who joined NEC later, it is pretty impressive to see that they were already at work discussing topics that we went on discussing ever after!

And wouldn't it have been fun to be there for the very first prototype demonstration ...

Although that first seminar set the basic pattern, much debate and planning went into subsequent ones. What needs had been spotted by executive members visiting classes? What would be useful both to refresh veterans and as orientation for new teachers? How could we develop greater ESL expertise? What could we do to raise the general awareness of community and race issues? What new directions should we take? How could we pass on new experiments and experience from outside NEC? What new materials were available?

It was also important not to make the day too high-powered or indigestible. The result of the debate was nearly always a mixed day – part of it spent on the nitty-gritty of classroom teaching, part on wider issues. Free time and space were always left for the participants to talk to one another, giving and getting support and renewed enthusiasm.

From the outset it was NEC policy that teachers should have had training and some experience in teaching English as a foreign or second language. This emphasis on professionalism was an important aspect of NEC and in the early seventies was in contrast with many local authority institutes and colleges which did not require TEFL/TESL training until some years later. Seminars were used to build up professionalism. We needed to supply our teachers with refresher training and briefings on new developments in the field. For these sessions we drew on experts and teacher-trainers from other organisations, as well as our own experienced teachers.

From the early days, Ruth and the other members of the executive had built up a strong relationship with International House, where Ruth, Katherine and many other NEC teachers received their grounding in TEFL techniques. The high standards of International House remained very valuable and relevant even when ESL became firmly established as a discipline in its own right. Many seminars were led by International House staff over the years and, interestingly

43

enough, quite a few of these trainers eventually moved across from EFL to ESL. One who did not, but who none the less made an outstanding contribution to NEC, was Joan Holby. She developed special links with us and not only led a number of seminars but also visited our classes and gave on-site training. There is no doubt that NEC owes a great deal to the unfailing support and unselfish generosity of Brita and John Haycraft of International House.

We also developed very helpful links with the Pathway Further Education Centre at Ealing (Southall) who shared their ESL expertise with us and gave their support and advice to many of our projects especially when we started our own programme of on-site in-service language training with a course for staff at University College Hospital. Several of our seminars were conducted by experts from Pathway both before and after the Industrial Language Training Unit was set up. Later we were also able to invite to our seminars members of the Inner London Industrial Language Training Units who gave very useful sessions.

ESL experts working in local education were very helpful, not only those in our own north-west London patch, but also those from south of the River and in the East End. Kundry Clarke, Judith Sansom, Margaret Hinchcliffe, Julia Naish, and Sue Freris are names that spring to mind. But co-operation and help from within ILEA really reached its high point after Westminster College of Further Education inaugurated their RSA course in TESL to Adult Immigrants under Sandra Nicholls' direction. Sandra herself gave one of the most memorable sessions ever – a surprise foreign language reading lesson. She gave it in Japanese, and several of NEC's own trainers subsequently took up the idea and gave lessons in written Gujerati, Urdu and Greek to home tutors and to local groups. The effect never failed to be salutary.

By no means all of our teachers were 'career' teachers. On the contrary, they came from a great variety of backgrounds – from medicine, music, social work, economics, journalism – not to mention raising families. Many joined us because they wanted to make a contribution to community relations, hoping through their work to promote a better acceptance of our new minorities. They wanted to help their students to adjust to life here, to deal with the difficulties and achieve a fair position in society. We ourselves offered a broad mix of British and foreign-born teachers and organisers, including many who belonged to the minority groups represented among our students.

44

To share our experiences and ideas and broaden the understanding of race and community issues, seminar discussions on these topics were regularly arranged. We found willing speakers from many quarters. Our closest community relations council, the CCCR of Camden, several times provided speakers on such diverse subjects as the general background of Cypriot immigrants in London, and the problem of harassment of and violence against Asians. Eric Jay, at that time the Camden Community Relations Organiser, opened constructive discussions on a couple of occasions, and Jenny Lo was a stimulating speaker after a showing of the film 'Singh 171' about the plight and problems of an Indian factory worker.

We had speakers from the CRC (later CRE), from community and advice centres, from the Hong Kong Government office, from the health services, the police and from many minority organisations. Pran Sheth, deputy chairman of the CRE, whose wife was a member of our executive committee, spoke more than once.* Much interest and concern was generated in our teachers and tutors by speakers on such health topics as the vitamin D shortage in many Asian diets, and the attitudes to family planning among our students.

NEC was precluded by its charitable status from taking any public political stand. We also feared increasing the risk of harassment of our vulnerable students in some areas; but a great deal of individual and grassroots work was done by our teachers and organisers. It cannot be said too often how deeply committed Ruth herself was, or how hard she worked for ideals.

For me, thinking back on seminars really means thinking back on my whole involvement with other NEC teachers and staff: and how much I enjoyed both my NEC work and the people I worked with. Ruth herself was an extraordinary boss – stimulating, demanding, inspiring, generous, impossible by turns! She loved to make openings and opportunities for people, and managed it for me as well as for so many others – making sure that my basic administrative work was balanced by the chance to participate in new projects, fieldwork, meetings and development work. We both loved seminars and they certainly brought out many aspects of our working relationship ... Ruth always drove me to them, even when they were virtually on our

* He was to express the appreciation which the CRE had for NEC in a long letter to Ruth which she read to the last seminar held in Camden in 1979.

doorstep at Gospel Oak. It was the best way of being sure I wouldn't be late! Once she realised that I was a congenitally bad time-keeper, she simply adapted to it with a shrug ...

In the early days I was always in a considerable panic on the way to a seminar, as I had probably forgotten the pins for the name tabs, or the float, or the notices, or the string (I never knew what it was for), or the sellotape, or the posters, and I expected to be taken to task for it!

But the morning fierceness was more than made up for by the generous and appreciative Ruth who emerged at the end of the day to drive me home and advise me to relax, thanking me warmly for whatever I had done, and enthusing all the way about speakers who had been lively or provocative, about teachers who were keen and committed (always speaking with special regard for NEC's loyal veterans, the 'golden oldies' as she called them), or about new ideas that had come up ... I hope no one was ever duped by her famous knitting into thinking that Ruth wasn't reading, marking, learning and inwardly digesting all that went on!

II

The first teaching materials produced were courses – not surprisingly, since a course is really the most fundamental item for the teacher. Most courses available on the open market at this time were geared to the quite different needs of students in intensive EFL colleges. In the early seventies Longman's Senior Scope courses were the only exception, and we therefore stocked and supplied them. Even so they had a limited application for our students.

In 1970 Marjorie Beadle drafted a 'structural' course especially for NEC. In 1974 we produced the Situational Course, drafted by a working party after groundwork had been done at one of our seminars. Finally, in 1975 we commissioned Marge Berer to write the Notional (i.e. functional) Course for us. This series of NEC courses reflected the new approaches to syllabus planning and language selection current in the TESL world at the time. They were all produced in summary form only – teachers' guides rather than teaching texts. Each one had its limitations, but taken together they offered constructive help and orientation for NEC teachers, particularly for those whose previous experience had been in straightforward TEFL.

In 1975, after a discussion during a seminar, we decided to

investigate the possibility of producing a fully fleshed-out text book. Sara Wood undertook to investigate whether there was enough homogeneity in the needs, language levels and interests of our 70-plus classes to make it feasible. In the event she decided that it was not. Although the idea was shelved, a number of excellent teaching ideas had come to light and these were collected together to form the basis of our 'teachers' pool' in the library.

Over the years NEC teachers have devised a number of special courses for particular projects. The workseekers' course, designed by Alan Shaffer for his classes of Ugandan Asian men in 1973; the hospital courses devised for the catering staff at University College Hospital by Tony Riley in 1974 and for domestic supervisors at St Mary's Hospital by Caroline Iffla in 1975/6. An ante-natal language pack was produced by Judith Nesbit in Hackney in 1977, and special programmes for Vietnamese refugees were developed by Gill Garb and Louise Morris at around the same time. A special programme for Chilean refugees was designed by Teresa Rogoyska also in 1977.

As for classroom materials, these were only produced if and when there really seemed to be a demand for them, and when there was nothing similar, appropriate or cheap enough on the open market. On the whole it seemed much more beneficial to hold seminar workshops on how to prepare or select materials, and then let individual teachers use their own initiative. Besides, we did not have sufficient funds to throw into classroom materials. A number of excellent projects came unstuck when production costs proved too high, perhaps most notably the Scope bingo game designed by Shirley Sadler Foster, which we could never afford to publish.

In 1975 a small group drafted some simple everyday dialogues which were recorded for us on tape by an International House team and proved popular. The longer set of situation dialogues (including how to make 999 calls) which we had made earlier were also very popular, though they were only available in written form.

We also produced two series of worksheets for students' writing practice, designed by Shirin Spencer. The first, consisting of basic name and address forms, job application forms, 'envelope' forms and fill-in clockfaces, have been perennially popular. The second, more ambitious, series, with picture stories and question-and-answer exercises, were useful in their way but lost ground as ESL expertise developed and teachers began to concentrate on more relevant functional literacy work. Also, by 1976/7, an excellent adult literacy pack, *Seven Days a Week*, had been produced by the Inner London Education Authority, and NEC invested in copies of this for every class instead of attempting to develop its own literacy materials.

So our collection of home-produced materials did gradually increase over the years, and NEC certainly remains indebted to the individuals and working parties who freely contributed their ideas, skill and time.

Whilst dealing with contributions in terms of materials, it is perhaps apposite to mention here the generosity of the writer L.G. Alexander who, in a welcome move which embodied a certain natural justice, dedicated to NEC the royalties on sales of his books in the Indian subcontinent.

III

Our classes were set up in a splendidly motley variety of places; the idea was always to take the classes to the students and not vice versa. As a result they were held in clinics, church halls, mosques, libraries, Chinese restaurants ... and clearly teachers working in such places needed a resource centre to which they could turn for books and equipment.

In 1975 NEC made two great steps in improving what it could offer teachers. First, we began to supply a standardised kit of basic equipment to all new teachers. This contained the NEC course, worksheets and other materials, flash cards, plastitak and chalk, a copy of the Scope Senior Course teacher's book and sample textbooks and, finally, an elementary collection of aids: a model telephone, large-print calendar, cardboard clockface and flipchart or posters.

Then we set up a display in our office where teachers could see both our own home-produced materials and our collection of books and materials from other sources. There were copies of materials produced by Pathway, Cambridge House and other language schemes, a fair-sized assortment of textbooks and readers, posters and wall charts from the health services, the Post Office, London Transport and the Royal Society for the Prevention of Accidents as well as from educational publishers; and background studies and journals from the Community Relations Commission and from the TEFL world. From this time, NEC was invited to send its mailing list to the CRC so that relevant journals and papers could be sent to our membership.

From 1971 onwards NEC had been at work building up a collection of portable cassette tape recorders for classroom use. The first batch were purchased with a generous grant of £500 from the Chandaria Foundation.

IV

A good measure of self-help and voluntary effort was called for from our teachers and most of them co-operated willingly. Headquarters supported all their efforts – and opprobrium fell upon those who didn't pull their weight! The main back-up items we produced were posters designed by Shirin Spencer, multi-lingual leaflets, which again dated from the early days of NEC, and postcards to send to students. The leaflets were in five Asian languages, and in Greek, Turkish and other European languages, as well as in Chinese and Arabic. They explained briefly what our classes had to offer and were usually overprinted with local class details.

Teachers also received frequent requests from their students for advice about housing, financial problems, children's schooling, etc; and for help in dealing with such difficulties as going into hospital, discrimination at work or racial attacks. We always recommended that they direct their students to the local professional advice service or CRC wherever possible, but we also kept a stock of leaflets on health, housing and citizens' rights in a number of languages. We also had a number of reference books on community and race issues, but most of the recurrent problems brought to our teachers were discussed at seminars where they were able to get advice on dealing with them.

It was not until we moved to 85a Highgate Road in 1975 that we had enough room to set up a proper library and expand our collection of loan items and reference materials. Most of the enormous task of cataloguing books and journals and monitoring supplies of leaflets and home-produced materials was undertaken by Hilary Paddon, who did an excellent job. She also set up card systems for both the reference and loan sections. New teachers were invited to 'at home' days when they could browse in the library at their leisure. The 'teachers' pool' contained not only solid good ideas but also quite inspired items such as the magazine written, illustrated and then printed at the NEC office by Jane Seigal's evening class in Brent.

Teachers borrowed wall charts and other visual aids, games, tapes and sets of readers, most of which were selected by our

working party on aids and materials, chaired by Rosemary Reid, which met from 1976 onwards. Rosemary did a lot of research and passed on her findings to our teachers in a couple of very useful seminar presentations.

The library was moved from Highgate Road to our next premises in Athlone Street and is now housed in the NEC Brent office.

At its peak, from a small office with a small staff, NEC ran an enormous teaching operation serving thousands of students. What funds there were, were channelled into running projects and doing fieldwork. Back-up services, such as the design and preparation of classroom materials, depended almost entirely on the good will of volunteers, and the rest of us remain grateful to all those who contributed their valuable time and talents.

The students

Indu Sheth

My first contact with Ruth was established through my husband. Ruth had kept in touch with him to discuss her thoughts from time to time on how she and all others who shared her care and concern could make the deprived and disadvantaged sections of society conscious of their rights, and how they might be taught to exercise them.

At one of these meetings, my husband suggested to her that since I was working amongst Asian immigrants to this country, and especially with Asian women, it might perhaps be a good idea for us to get together.

Early in 1971 Ruth and I met and the first seeds of Neighbourhood English Classes in the Wembley area were sown. Ruth and I agreed that not only Asian but all other non-English-speaking immigrants – Cypriots, Chinese, Turks, Poles, Greeks, etc. – needed help to learn the English language which would make it easier for them to cope with their day-to-day needs.

It was over a cup of coffee at Ruth's flat that we planned to start Neighbourhood English Classes in Wembley. We discussed in detail how to persuade and encourage adult immigrants to join these classes, where the classes should be located, how to acquire suitable premises and how to recruit teachers with an interest in, and an understanding of, teaching students who had practically no knowledge of the English language.

Within three weeks of that momentous discussion and decision, I started my work for the enrolment of students.

Every evening after dinner, accompanied by my son Sunil who was then only 14 years old, I went around those areas of Wembley where there was a concentration of immigrants. We would knock on doors and enquire whether there were any people who would like to learn English. A mixed response greeted us. Some women would listen to us with incredulity. Others, the more curious ones, thought it was a good idea to learn the language but wanted

52

to consult their husbands first. And still others, who worked in factories or had some other menial job, immediately welcomed the idea; they realised from their own experience the additional problems they were encountering because of their lack of knowledge of the language.

During one of these many visits to individual homes, I was fortunate enough to make the acquaintance of Jaya Chouhan, an acquaintance which turned into a lasting friendship between Jaya, Ruth and me. Jaya immersed herself enthusiastically in the work of enrolling and organising students and classes.

Ruth and I met very frequently, and I informed her of my experiences with different households. In consequence we prepared a written brief which Jaya and I could use whenever we called at any immigrant home. The gist of this brief was to convince prospective students that if they had some knowledge of English, they would be better able to understand and appreciate the laws of this country and their own civil rights and responsibilities. In addition, they would be able to discuss their children's progress with the teachers when they visited their children's schools. They would learn enough to explain their physical ailments to their doctors, and in case of emergency they would be able to call an ambulance or the police. It would help them with their shopping, at the post office, and in the use of public transport.

In short, it would make it easier for them to lead their daily lives in the totally foreign environment outside their homes.

The immigrants were having a difficult time and they realised that here was an opportunity they could grasp. Slowly they started to recognise that command of basic English would help them in many ways.

One of the problems we encountered was the feeling amongst the students that it would be impossible for an English teacher who did not know the immigrants' mother tongue to teach English to immigrants who did not know a word of English. Some suggested I should teach them. Others expressed willingness to join the classes, but on condition that I remained in the classroom while they were being taught by English teachers. In order to reassure them I agreed to remain in the room, and in the early days I became part of the class myself.

On several occasions small group meetings of prospective students were held in private homes. Ruth and I attended these together, and her sincerity and total commitment proved to be reassuring to some of the more sceptical.

The first English class under the aegis of NEC was established at the Methodist Church in Park Lane, Wembley. Shirin Spencer and Betty Jacobs were the first teachers. On the opening day, the students were warmly welcomed and courteously treated and soon understood that the fact that they did not know English did not render them inadequate in any way.

The teaching began and with every day that passed the confidence of those attending the classes, and others who had come simply to observe, increased. One week after commencing the classes, over 30 new students turned up for enrolment. Ruth and I were staggered by this phenomenal increase, but were pleased to see that our efforts were beginning to succeed.

The vast increase in numbers presented its own problems. Ruth and I started rushing around to find more accommodation for additional classes, for more teachers and for further resources. The movement had truly caught on. My telephone was ringing at all hours, more and more people were inquiring about classes. Young and old, men and women, wanted more information. The demand for classes in the neighbourhood multiplied and so did the activities which Ruth and I had to undertake to organise them. We were in almost daily contact to discuss ways and means of improving our organisation, promoting further interest and encouraging those who were already attending classes.

Of course, the students themselves often had their own personal problems, and at times problems between students and teachers arose from language difficulties and mutual misunderstandings. At practically no notice at all, I often had to rush out to deal with them at the request of either the student or the teacher.

As interest in the classes grew, the students themselves, with the assistance of their teachers, began other activities – such as celebrating Divali, Christmas and the Navratri festivals. The Wembley class organised a bring-and-buy sale in aid of disabled children. I remember that at this first sale the handsome sum of £137 was collected and presented to the Mayor of Brent who accepted it as a noble gesture on the part of students and teachers of NEC.

There then followed day trips, organised on the initiative of the students and teachers, to various parts of London and to places of interest outside London. This was an important step forward in familiarising the students, their families and their friends with the life, culture and traditions of this country and its people.

After the success of Wembley, Ruth and I, with the assistance of many others, started major drives for new classes in Willesden

Green, Neasden, Kilburn and Harlesden. An almost door-to-door search for students commenced. In some of the streets we knocked on almost every door enquiring whether there were any immigrant families living there. Some of the white residents would direct us helpfully by telling us, 'Go to the third house' or 'There is a family in Number 22'.

Through such 'cold' canvassing more contacts were developed, more students enrolled. Initially the response came from the women alone, but then suddenly we found that men, too, were interested in joining the classes. In the early stages there were doubts whether Asian women, because of their traditional modesty and shyness, would wish to be in the same class with men, but the barriers were soon brought down. Their shyness evaporated like morning dew, and genuine fellow-feeling developed among all students learning the new language, in co-operation with each other, drawing support and help from each other. A new and healthy self-confidence was emerging.

With the enormous success of 30 classes dotted all over the borough of Brent behind us, we directed our attention to Harrow. Here there was a substantial Pakistani community and we felt that we must make a beginning with Pakistani women by drawing them out to join our classes. Ruth entrusted me with this task and responsibility. I got in touch with the chairman of a Pakistani organisation in Harrow.

The chairman, Mr Chaudhury, was a highly energetic person and he enthusiastically welcomed NEC's initiative. Through him I obtained a list of a large number of Pakistani women living in Harrow. Accompanied by Mr Chaudhury, I spent many days visiting over a hundred homes and personally explaining to my Pakistani sisters the need and advantages of their joining English classes. Most of their husbands worked on night shifts and consequently during the daytime visits to their wives I was able also to meet the husbands. They did not appear to be very keen on their wives joining our classes. When we finally started our first regular class in Harrow, out of the hundred or so families we had visited, we had only two Pakistani women students. Most discouraging and depressing, both for Ruth and myself, as well as for Mr Chaudhury, but we did not give up. Although success with Pakistani women was limited, the Harrow classes evoked considerable response from many other sections of the immigrant community. (Nowadays very many Pakistani women attend local ESL classes.)

Right from the start, Ruth and I were very conscious of the

numerous hurdles in persuading immigrant women to come forward and join the neighbourhood classes. Attitudes had to be changed, suspicions eradicated, traditional taboos removed and a sense of purpose and confidence inculcated. Ruth was a great source of inspiration and a tireless missionary. She was a relentless campaigner. Her strength of character and her boundless determination kept me and the others going.

As I look back on those early and very exciting years of the NEC, and my association and activities with Ruth, I cannot but feel a deep sense of fulfilment. NEC is a fitting monument to the memory of Ruth Hayman. I feel proud that I have been in some measure associated with it.

A noise in my ears ... and squiggles

Kumud Banarse

I was about nine when I came to England from India. I did not know the English language or anything about the country except what I had imagined – which was just complete fantasy.

Within a few weeks of my being here and just as I was becoming familiar with the new surroundings, one cold December day I was rushed off to hospital for an emergency appendicitis operation. It was a traumatic experience which I have never forgotten. I remember the nurses and doctors being very kind, but it was the black mask that frightened and angered me most. I'm sure the nurse must have explained what it was for – but not knowing a syllable of English, I suppose I just didn't understand. All I can remember is the nurse placing this horrid-looking black rubber mask on my face and me violently protesting verbally by saying 'nahi-nahi' in Marathi (my mother-tongue), and physically pushing it away.

There were to be many experiences, but the most significant which I feel might have had some influence on my later interest in ESL was perhaps when I went to my first school in England. This was quite soon after the operation. Again, I recall the teachers and children being very sympathetic and kind. The children were just fascinated by me; it was quite obvious that this was the first Indian they had come across. Anyway, whatever they were saying to me was just a noise in my ears, and when it came to reading and writing, they appeared just like squiggles. However, it was lucky for me that I was a child, because within a year I managed to learn to speak, read and write – although not well enough to pass the 11+ the following year!

It was a different story for my mother, though – as a forward-looking young widow, tired of the oppressive life for women and especially for widows in India, she decided to make a fresh start and she chose to do this in 'Wilayat' – England. There were more opportunities here for women – but not for a non-English-speaking, sari-clad Indian woman without work experience.

After endless rejections, Mother decided that the next job she applied for she would say that she had had experience – and to everybody's joy, the trick worked and Mother found herself working as a machinist in a clothing factory. This is where she really started learning her English, although she used to attend evening classes as well.

Finding work was not the only problem she had to overcome, she also had to learn how to cope with the local community. For instance, she was not aware that she could claim family allowance, put her name down for a council place, etc., which, if she had known, would have made life a little easier raising two young children. Watching Mother struggle (not necessarily understanding why) was sad and hard but an invaluable experience which will always be with me.

...And these are the memories that came flooding to my mind when a friend told me of a poster in the local library asking for volunteers to teach English on a one-to-one basis in the home.

So, in February 1976, when the youngest of my three children was settled at school, I started as a NEC home tutor.

After a few months I was helping as a voluntary classroom assistant, and by then I had discovered a taste for teaching so I enrolled for the RSA TESL course. During the course, in January 1977, I was fortunate enough to be offered an NEC evening class in Harrow, just around the corner from where I lived.

At this time I had the opportunity to meet Ruth Hayman, who was to interview me, and by the end of the interview I just felt a great urge to thank her for the marvellous work she was doing for the Asian community – though I felt I didn't really know her well enough to do this. I took a deep breath and with great trepidation blurted out my say. I am sure that Ruth must have been thanked a million times, but I consider myself fortunate and privileged to have had the opportunity to say 'thank you' to a person of great character and strength who will always be remembered.

The following year, in 1978, I also started teaching NEC classes in Brent. One of them was the Barnhill Road Nursery class, a typical NEC class, quite large, mixed ability and mixed age group. It was a friendly group, and besides learning English we found that we were discussing various topics from personal and domestic problems to current affairs. It dawned on me that the so-called English class seemed to be fulfilling social needs as well as linguistic ones, and that clearly these students needed something between the English class and the Satsang (a religious gathering), a kind of get-together group for women of all ages. I put forward the idea to the class and was pleased at the enthusiastic response.

For support I approached one of the first NEC students, Pushpa Patel. She agreed that something like this was needed and together, with the help of the students, we started Milan, a friendly get-together group. The matron of Barnhill Road Nursery kindly let us use the premises one afternoon a month, without charge. After a couple of meetings the group began to gel and we discussed finding premises with more facilities for cookery demonstrations, a children's corner, et.

I made several enquiries regarding this project, but not being experienced in these matters and not having the right contacts, I did not succeed. I was very disappointed, aware that there was a need for a group of this kind and yet not being able to get support. Having put in quite a lot of time, I felt I could not do more and unfortunately the Milan group began to die a slow death – but not for long. In 1983 a local government grant was given to start four Milan Club projects in Brent, and I am glad to say they are all flourishing.

On looking back I feel that being an Asian and speaking Hindi was certainly a great advantage to me. Even though most of my students were Gujerati, they felt they could relate to me and without doubt this helped to cement the bond between teaching and personal relationships.

It gave me great pleasure to see my students not only progressing linguistically but also growing in confidence in other ways. NEC has certainly had some influence on my life and without doubt on many of my students' lives as well – even though some of them may not realise it. It has certainly filled a great need and has much to be thanked for.

When Rose retired as home tutor organiser in 1982 I applied for the post and was delighted to be appointed. It was time for a change after five years of teaching and I looked forward to the challenge.

I find it quite incredible looking back to know that for me it all began seven years ago, when I first volunteered to be a home tutor.

I understand the feelings of mute people

Pushpa Patel

26-1-83

Dear Mrs Rose Grant
I send you my experiences and the influence on me of Neighbourhood English Classes. I remember the day when we first met. Always you had a smiling face. You also encouraged me to progress. If we hadn't had the late Miss Ruth Hayman, we would not have met one another. We are grateful to everyone connected with NEC. My kind regards to you and your family. Thank you very much for encouraging us to study English. There is no age limit to studying anything. Please, forgive my mistakes. Thank you again.

Yours sincerely,
Pushpa Patel

My name is Pushpa Patel. I came from Nairobi (Kenya, East Africa) to London on the 8th of May 1971.

I learned English in my mother country, India. Even though I had difficulty in understanding the pronunciations.

I could not speak English everywhere where I needed it. That's why I understand the difficulties and the feelings of mute people.

When I came here, it was summer. I found apple blossoms, beautiful roses and other flowers in the gardens. The days were very long so it was amazement to me. I enjoyed visiting various gardens and historical places. In the beginning I had a problem in speaking with other people and understanding them.

One day I met a friend who was from Kenya. She asked me to join her English class. I was so delighted and asked her 'Where?' She told me 'It is in Park Lane, at the Methodist Church, Wembley.' It was not far from my house, only fifteen or twenty minutes walk. So I decided to go with her to the English class. When I went to the class, she first introduced me to the teacher.

I started to study English on the 14th February 1972. Our teacher was Mrs Betty Jacobs. She gave me a test to know at what stage I was. I was able to study the book 'English – Situational Part II'. So she gave it to me.

In the beginning I could read and write but could not understand when my teacher spoke. One day she gave us some homework from the book but I did not do it even though I had a lot of time! I went to the class without homework. My teacher asked me politely, 'Pushpa, why didn't you do your homework?' I answered her truthfully that I did not understand about homework. She found out what my difficulty was – that I could not understand the pronunciations. After that she always wrote our homework on the black board and let us know which the exercise was and what page it was on in the book. I was successful in doing the homework by that method.

I could read properly from the book but could not speak fluently because I was afraid I would make mistakes in speaking. When my classmates were talking to our teacher, I only listened to their conversation. This was another problem. One day she asked us to bring some souvenirs and we had to tell her about the souvenirs, where we got them from. I am a collector of beautiful thoughts and unusual things. I went to class with many such things and talked about them in detail. Slowly I got confidence in speaking. Always teachers are helpful in understanding and solving the students' problems.

There were friendly classmates from different countries in our class. So I had the opportunity to learn about their customs and cultures from them. Every summer three or four combined classes went on various trips by coach with the teachers. We also enjoyed all Christmas parties at Christmas times, which included bring and buy, dancing, Christmas carols and *garba* (Gujerati folk dance). We also invited our organisers, the Mayor and other well-known persons.

I studied English for five years with Mrs Betty Jacobs. The second teacher was Kathy Gelb, the third teacher was Mrs Alison Benstead and the present teacher is Jane Siegel. I've learned their various methods of teaching.

I have been a volunteer assistant since 1975. I very much enjoy helping the beginners. I made many friends amongst teachers, students and other people connected with Neighbourhood English Classes. My sincere thanks to all those who are connected with NEC, especially to the late Miss Ruth Hayman. I am sincerely grateful to NEC.

Our aim – to work ourselves out of a job

Shirley Sadler Forster

Home tutoring in North London started as an off-shoot of the Cambridge House scheme in South London. There was at first no training for home tutors, and no teaching materials; we could speak English and with a minimal briefing we went to teach it to women who had recently arrived in this country. Some tutors were probably quite good; at the worst they did no harm, and at the best discovered a latent talent for teaching. In most cases the tutor's role was as much friend as teacher and we found ourselves helping with a variety of students' problems.

My own experience as a home tutor in Camden in 1970 was probably typical. Mother of three school-age children, I was doing several interesting voluntary jobs while trying to decide what would be the right sort of paid work.

It was with some trepidation that, totally untrained and with no teaching experience, I went to see my first student. With good will on both sides, and fortunately some knowledge of English on her part, we had a happy first session getting to know each other. She lived in one very cramped room and it was clear that I would have to bring something for her small boy to play with if we were going to be able to concentrate on our next lesson.

I turned up the following week, armed with lego and stacking cups, to be told that my student had got a job. I was extremely disappointed, and sorry that she had not been able to avail herself of the opportunity to improve her English. However a second student was soon found and my relationship with her lasted for several years. She had learned some English at school, and our lessons consisted of my correcting her mistakes in conversation and helping her to read. Very unsatisfactory by today's standards, but in fact help with her English was probably one of the less important areas of my support. She had come to England with two small daughters and a baby boy.

Everything was new to her and there were the usual difficulties over housing (the family had one bed-sitting room) and schools. I could sympathise when her father died, so far away; we took an interest in each other's children, went on outings together and I hope that, at the very least, the friendship of one English woman made settling here a little easier.

With the increase in immigration, and a growing awareness that where EFL classes existed they were not suitable for most of the new arrivals, the teaching of ESL emerged as a separate discipline. Along with the establishment of community classes, NEC started home tutor schemes in adjoining boroughs: Brent, Harrow, Hackney, Islington and Barnet. The first NEC part-time paid organisers were appointed in 1974 and the first training course for home tutors was run at the Marylebone Institute in October 1974. From then on, training was normally available for our home tutors, even if it sometimes meant that they had to travel to other boroughs.

In July of 1974 an NEC home tutor organisers' committee was started and as new organisers were appointed, the committee grew. The topics we discussed were very similar to those which concern organisers today – problems of recruiting tutors, the design of posters and leaflets, the need for a kit or course-book for tutors. The committee explored the possibility of advertising in Indian cinemas (no), and considered the need for tutors' identity cards (no).

Money was a constant preoccupation and there were repeated applications for financial help to local authorities and charities, and for urban aid.

Requests for local or central government funds were rarely successful at the first attempt and a lot of time was spent, particularly by Ruth, on budgets and discussions about pay scales, and whether tutors' travelling expenses could be reimbursed – but very few tutors asked for this.

In no two boroughs was NEC's provision the same. Not only did the distribution of students vary, but relationships with borough and community relations councils differed, as did the availability of committed people keen to work with us. In most boroughs NEC ran home tutor schemes *and* classes, with more or less help from the local authority. Close links between tutors and classroom teachers were considered essential. Right from the start, home tutoring was seen as a preparation for class attendance, and tutors were encouraged to take their students to classes as soon as they were ready.

The home tutor organisers' committee continued to meet but, with the growth of NEC commitments, there was concern that the executive committee was losing touch with the organisers. Consequently, in 1975 we were asked to attend enlarged meetings of the executive once a month – marathon meetings which some of us dreaded, but which did prove worthwhile. At that time most home tutor organisers also attended their borough co-ordinating committees on which representatives of the borough council, the local community relations council and other interested bodies served.

As local authorities steadily assumed more responsibility the role of NEC contracted. All the boroughs where NEC was once involved now have a home tutor organiser (though not all are full-time) and some clerical help, funded either by the local authority or by urban aid.

Today's schemes are similar to those started more than ten years ago, though there are some differences. The original student was usually a shy beginner and the tutor's aim was to help her gain sufficient confidence and enough basic English to join a class.

Now the majority of students have been in the country for a few years but, because they often live in a close-knit community, they have not felt the need to improve their command of English. Others cannot attend a class because there is a new baby to look after, or there is no class near enough to home. Until very recently a growing number of women had full-time jobs and often had language needs in connection with their work, but their domestic responsibilities made classroom attendance out of the question, and so they needed a home tutor in the evenings.

During the 1970s volunteering became far more highly organised, and volunteer bureaux were established in most boroughs. The concept of 'doing good' became somewhat outmoded, and it was seen that one's reasons for volunteering were only partly altruistic.

Some volunteers seek to fill the gap left by diminishing family responsibilities, some have always wanted to teach or are themselves members of a formerly immigrant and persecuted minority, such as the Jews. Others look for a satisfying and useful occupation during early retirement or a period of unemployment.

A number of volunteers have always hoped that their voluntary work might lead to a career, and the recent RSA Preparatory Certificate in teaching English as a second language to adults offers a valuable way in.

Concerned about problems of race riots, immigration acts, police harassment and National Front activities, many people look for some way of making a practical contribution to good community relations. Home-tutoring is such a way and the spin-off in terms of mutual understanding should not be underestimated. Quite apart from the enjoyment of teaching, tutors invariably say how interesting and rewarding they find the contact with a family from one of the minority ethnic groups.

Community relations councils are playing an increasingly important role, and community consciousness has grown. The home tutor organiser is an essential link in a multi-ethnic community. She is in touch with health, social, education and other services, and through her home tutors she can pass on information which might otherwise not reach isolated students. She can identify local needs, whether for ante-natal exercises, playgroups, or simply somewhere where elderly members of minority groups can meet. As local initiatives get off the ground, she can help to ensure that local members of minority groups are not left out.

The support which home tutors receive has increased enormously over the years. All organisers now provide a basic training course which starts with a demonstration lesson in a foreign language, gives some information about students' backgrounds, and helps tutors to look at language from the point of view of helping communication rather than perfecting grammar.

There are regular newsletters and follow-up seminars on topics such as the use of cassette recorders or the teaching of writing, and informal get-togethers when tutors exchange ideas and discuss their problems. The organiser keeps in touch by telephone and, as well as the introductory kit, provides a range of suitable materials from which to choose items relevant to individual students.

There are fewer new arrivals now. Many of those who do come have some English, but the young women still have before them several years at home with small children; they are glad of the opportunity to improve their English, often with a view to enhancing their prospects when they are ready to return to work outside the home.

Older people, who have in the past relied on having a relative on hand to interpret, are beginning to realise that this is not always possible, and to fear being cut off from their

English-speaking grandchildren. Their slower learning speed may mean that a home tutor is more effective for them than having to struggle with the faster pace of the class. And periodic influxes of refugees produce yet more students.

So, although our aim must be to work ourselves out of a job, its realisation is still far off.

Tools for home tutors

Rose Grant

Most volunteer ESL home tutors come raw to the job. They have had no training and, usually, no experience of any kind of teaching, let alone the teaching of our rich and at times baffling English language. Depending upon their temperaments, they are either eager to have a go, or else terrified at the enormity of their self-chosen responsibility.

How did NEC home tutor organisers enable – or try to enable – these novices to prepare themselves?

What training, what guidelines, what teaching-learning aids did we offer – and with what success?

The first NEC organisers were almost as much in the dark as were the volunteers: together we embarked upon a process of trial and error. It lasted for many years, and is still not completed. Not only did the tutors want to find out what to teach, and how to teach it (a lifelong study anyway), they also needed to know something about the background of the ethnic minority families into whose homes they would be going, and what their role as once-a-week visitors would be.

Some of this could be and was touched on when a home tutor organiser first met and briefed a new recruit, giving her – for most were women – the home tutor kit and arranging for her to attend the next local training course.

These courses were held once or twice each term, on a day and at a time convenient for the majority of attenders, usually for six to eight sessions of two hours each in consecutive weeks. Sometimes, if the volunteers were still at school or university, the times were adjusted to meet special needs.

Some ESL schemes were already experimenting with the training of ESL home tutors as early as 1970, but the NEC courses did not begin until the autumn of 1974. The first was a joint Camden-Brent undertaking, with Ann Herschmann for Camden and Rose Grant for Brent as the original NEC part-time paid organisers. Rosanne Balfour, a teacher experienced in ESL

69

This Home Tutor Kit was written by Margot Firkin in conjunction with an NEC working party. The Kit was published by the Council for Racial Equality and was in great demand from its first appearance in February 1977. It was reprinted several times.

A new Kit, produced by a NATESLA working party, is in preparation.

WELCOME !

Now that you have become a volunteer
home tutor, we intend to do everything
we can to give you all the support and
assistance you need.

We hope that this kit, and the training
course, will prove helpful, but remember
that the Home Tutor Organiser is there
to assist both you and your student.
Please consult her if you have any
problems and worries.

Your first visit to your student will be
the start of a new friendship for you
both, and, though you are there to help
your student to achieve an improvement
in her English, you will find that you
are not only giving, but gaining -
gaining an insight into another culture,
gaining an extension of your own
experience, and gaining what can be a
most rewarding new relationship.

*(Throughout this kit we adopted the convention
of referring to the student as 'she' though
we are aware that students are frequently male.)*

SAMPLE 1977 HOME TUTOR TRAINING COURSE PROGRAMME

(Courses usually consist of one two-hour session per week for
six consecutive weeks. Tutors are asked to bring their home
tutor kit with them to each session.)

    Session 1

    MEETING EACH OTHER
    LESSON IN A FOREIGN LANGUAGE
    DISCUSSION
    TEACHING AND LEARNING - some do's and don'ts

    Session 2

    THE ENGLISH OUR STUDENTS NEED
    PATTERNS IN THE LANGUAGE AND HOW TO TEACH THEM

    Session 3

    USE OF PICTURES
    DIALOGUES
    PROPS AND AIDS FOR YOUR DIALOGUES
    PRONUNCIATION

    Session 4

    WORKSHOP : PREPARED DIALOGUES
    READING AND WRITING

    Session 5

    READING AND WRITING MATERIALS
    WORKSHOP : PLANNING A LESSON
    WHAT NEXT? A home-made syllabus or a coursebook?

    Session 6

    YOUR COMPLETE TEACHING PACK FOR A LESSON
    DISCUSSION : LONG TERM AIMS
    REVIEW OF THE COURSE

for adults, was our counsellor and guide and was tutor-in-charge of the new course.

What a lot we tried to cram into our new volunteers! Far too much! One of the Brent contingent, a senior nurse who had herself trained nursing recruits, wanted to resign half-way through. 'Too difficult,' she complained. 'Can't take it all in.' We persuaded her to stay, and she proved to be a splendid home tutor.

But the overloading of the course syllabus was a persistent problem. To keep abreast with the current theory and practice of ESL teaching, and to adapt it for one-to-one purposes, the pattern of our programmes had frequently to be changed. We introduced more group discussion, with question-and-answer periods – and more workshops, more use of audio-visual aids, more self-questioning of our aims and the quality of our service, more awareness of our ethnic minority students, their needs and expectations, and their recourse to mother-tongue communication.

NEC class teachers who liked the idea of becoming trainers of home tutors, were invited to sit in on a training course, and several of them added this to their skills, becoming trainers themselves.

Three major Ruth-inspired initiatives made 1976 an outstanding year. Early in January we called together an NEC work party to devise a model course for home tutors. Called 'A Framework for Home Tutor Training Courses – a Blueprint prepared by NEC', it was published by the Community Relations Council and widely distributed.

The same work party, plus a representative from the Commission for Racial Equality Education Department, and several other invited experts, met many times that year for hectic assessment of the most effective contents of a new home tutor kit. It saw the light of day at last, in 1977, and has since been reprinted many times in editions of thousands. As Ruth recalled in her NEC Chairman's Report for 1976 and 1977:

The pre-1976 home tutor kit consisted of a variety of teaching aids, worksheets, book lists, tips on lesson planning and suggestions on teaching techniques. It was certainly some help to tutors, but was very difficult to use as the items were unrelated and had been collected together without any overall planning.

The NEC/CRE Work Party considered that the best way to produce a coherent new kit was to have the material (after it had been selected and edited) rewritten in a uniform style by one person.

Margot Firkin was commissioned to do the rewriting and worked in close contact with the Work Party. Suitable illustrations were subsequently added and the CRC (now CRE) produced the kit which has been well received and is now in general use throughout the country.

Margot Firkin, a senior lecturer in the Harrow ESL scheme, did a difficult job extremely well, and refused the fee allocated for her work.

The third notable event of 1976 was the pilot project instigated by Ruth for a series of seminars designed to train home tutor trainers and home tutor organisers. Up until then, effective trainers had remained uncomfortably scarce, worth their weight in gold – but nobody weighed them.

A small planning team from NEC, CRE and Waltham Forest College began their preparatory work in February. Three months later the course was opened in Central London, funded by CRE and attended by ESL teachers and home tutor organisers from London and the south-east. At least eight of them became home tutor trainers.

NEC prepared a comprehensive report on this training which was issued by the CRE. Fascinating – and instructive.

Nowadays, and for the past several years, the handbook 'Training the Trainers', compiled by a group of ILEA experts, is much used and a new home tutor kit, devised by the CRE, is about to be published.

The telephone rang ...
and rang ... and rang ...

Joyce Morton

My involvement with NEC began in January 1972 when I replied to a short advertisement in the South Highgate Parents Club Bulletin for part-time secretarial/book-keeping work. Subsequently, my involvement expanded and changed as NEC developed. In due course I became chief administrative officer and served on the executive committee in turn as hon. treasurer and hon. secretary.

The non-hierarchical structure of NEC, coupled with the very special personality of Ruth Hayman and those who joined NEC, and the urgency and rapid expansion of the work, inspired a special kind of loyalty and enthusiasm. A high degree of professionalism was always demanded – perhaps because of Ruth's legal training and background – and, because we were spending public money, record keeping, budgets, letters to local authorities, teachers' contracts and publicity material were all dealt with as scrupulously as they would have been had we been a much larger organisation.

By February 1972 NEC had officially been in existence for two years – the first committee minutes are dated April 1970. Our constitution was ratified in November 1972. We were then registered as a charity by the Department of Education and Science and were free to raise funds to support our work. Ruth and Katherine dealt with all the correspondence and affairs of the new organisation from Ruth's flat. The telephone seemed to ring endlessly. Immaculately kept files were stored in the spare room. One small ledger was sufficient to record our financial affairs.

At last in May 1972 we were offered office space by the Camden Council of Social Services – a large upstairs room in the Neighbourhood Advice Centre in Malden Road, Kentish Town, rent-free for the first year and subsequently at £2 a week. We bought our office furniture second-hand, installed a telephone, and shared duplicating facilities with the other community groups using the premises.

Tony Riley was appointed for a one-year period as our first Language Organiser at a salary of £2000 per annum. He was responsible for preparing material for on-site in-service language courses at University College Hospital. Caroline Iffla began to work full-time for NEC, combining the roles of secretary/teacher/administrator in NEC's usual way. Shortly thereafter, a grant from the British Council of Churches enabled us to re-define her job and she was engaged as teacher/organiser from April 1974. The administrative work mushroomed as classes (now numbering approximately 50 in ten inner and outer London boroughs) grew and pioneer projects were started. A home tutor sub-committee was formed in June of that year, and was administered from headquarters.

In August 1974 a hasty departure from Malden Road became necessary with the unwelcome news that the building was structurally unsafe! Everything was packed up and moved back to Ruth's flat – now our materials filled her garage as well as her spare room. Eventually we found a room in a disused shop front in the Highgate Road. Downstairs MENCAP had its toy library, used only in the evenings. For nine months, while help from Camden Council and many other sources was sought, NEC's rapidly growing work was carried on here in far from ideal conditions. Our honorary auditor, Roger Tabakin, suggested we engage a part-time book-keeper because involvement with trusts and urban aid grants was increasing, so in January 1975 our first book-keeper was appointed, to be replaced a year later by Hazel Scarr. She has been with us ever since, assuming an ever wider range of responsibilities.

In 1975 the City Parochial Foundation agreed to fund the appointment of an office manager, part-time, for three years. Later that year we heard of a short-term occupancy in Camden and in the summer, Dorothy and Roger Levy (she was to become our first office manager) helped make the new premises ready. We stayed in these 'temporary' quarters for nearly two years. One of the rooms was used to display books and materials for our teachers and tutors to inspect and borrow. In the other room, clerical and administrative work was done. We served coffee to all comers, and a staff member or a member of the executive committee was always on hand to advise teachers and students. Hilary Padden and Caroline arranged the reference library and our supply of teaching aids and materials was much augmented. The 1975 Annual Report says, 'at last NEC has a headquarters ...'.

It had always been part of NEC's philosophy to decentralise and now we began to put this into effect. The first NEC part-time home tutor organisers/language co-ordinators were Ann Herschmann in Camden and Rose Grant in Barnet, appointed in early summer 1974. A year later Gul-Anaar Kanji was appointed in Harrow, and in December 1975 Ann Hettich became the full-time local organiser in Brent.

Now we decided that more funds were needed to finance short-term appointments and area offices. The office manager's post was relinquished and we asked Marge Berer to write a special teaching course for NEC, Rosemary Reid to produce special teaching aids and materials for us and Annie Millet to act as part-time child helper organiser. In addition, NEC helped to support home tutor organisers in Hackney (first Sue Lucas, then Juliet Ash and finally Sabrina Aaronovitch held this post), originally with the help of the local Community Relations Committees.

By 1977 our need for permanent office accommodation had become acute. We wanted to stay within the Camden borders and we could certainly not afford a commercial rent. Through good friends we heard that the Camden branch library in Athlone Street, West Kentish Town, was moving to new premises and within days of applying for a lease we were accepted as new tenants. We had hoped to share with another charity, but in the end assumed full responsibility ourselves. Camden charged us a rent we could afford and generously granted us 100 per cent rate relief. All the necessary legal and architectural advice and work was given to us free of charge. We made extensive alterations to the library rooms. Six months after we moved in, ACORN, a social services project funded by the Manpower Services Committee, became our co-tenants.

Two busy and eventful years followed. Though the local authorities took responsibility for more and more classes and home tutoring, the co-ordination of our expanding organisation still stemmed from the centre. When the Brent organiser married and resigned her post, NEC headquarters administered most of the ESL language work in Brent until approaches to the Brent Education Committee by the executive committee met with a sympathetic response, and in January 1980 John Fitzpatrick was appointed Brent ESL language organiser.

While we were searching for a new office for the Brent area, it became obvious that a long-term commitment to bricks and mortar was inappropriate for NEC. ILEA had taken over responsibility for all the work in the inner London boroughs (including, of course, Camden) and language organisers were appointed by the authority. Our main link with ESL classes was through our child helpers. Luckily we had not yet signed a formal lease for the Athlone Street premises and when the Camden Committee for Community Relations needed a place for their Springboard team, we decided to sublet part of our space.

Eventually we handed the premises back to Camden Council in October 1980. All the administrative work (except that for finances, which Hazel took home with her) moved back to Ruth's flat. Because of this decision we were able to increase our financial support for the new Brent office. They also inherited much of our office furniture. Some was also given to Harrow and to the Barnet Home Tutor Scheme.

We continued to administer NEC from Ruth's flat until her untimely and sad death in October 1981. Since then, all the central files have been moved to my house where the massive minute books record the progress of NEC over 13 fruitful years. Here, too, are kept the index of charities and supporting trusts, the financial reports, the class lists, the seminar reports, and the reports of the child helpers, the home tutors and the summer projects, as well as the many press articles reporting the extraordinary development of NEC from the seed sown by Ruth and Katherine in 1970.

Our executive committee still meets regularly and committee members undertake a varied work load as volunteers. We continue to provide a skeleton back-up for the committee, liaison with the remaining local co-ordinating committees, and financial oversight of those urban aid grants for which we are partly responsible.

Many of the able local organisers now working all over London began their careers with NEC. How can we be less than proud of our part in the development of ESL in London?

A rare and much
sought-after animal

by the secretary of a charitable trust

NEC is fun. Fun from the first class I saw Caroline Iffla give, to the latest meeting of the executive committee. It has always clearly been a coming-together of people who enjoy immensely what they're doing, enjoy each other's company and, I think in no small way as a consequence of that, do what they do very well indeed.

I didn't know NEC in its beginnings in Ruth Hayman's flat. When I first came to know it (through Ruth and the Lomans Trust, which my Trustees had already supported for some years) it was already in short-life accommodation in Highgate Road – premises of a kind so familiar to trust administrators who work with small innovatory voluntary organisations. Before long it had moved to much larger premises in Athlone Street – the Old Library – where there was room for seminars, meetings and the library, as well as the administration. And then in two years it was back in Ruth's flat. This progression of premises is important because it is symbolic of something that makes NEC rather unusual.

From very small beginnings one or two people who saw a need and a way to help others, drew in more like-minded people and gradually built up a large and efficient organisation. They provided not only English classes for immigrants throughout much of North London and beyond, but also home tutoring and help with the children who were brought to the classes by their mothers. By the way, as it were, NEC also contributed substantially to the establishment of a body of qualified teachers who now have their own professional organisation. As time went on and local authorities took over responsibility for the classes NEC bowed out, retaining involvement only for those classes and services which would not otherwise have been provided.

Perhaps NEC was fortunate in its timing; if it had started in

1980 rather than in 1970 it is unlikely that the local authorities would have been able to take over its work. For the grant-making trust this is a rare and much sought-after animal – a voluntary body that identifies a need and meets it with the aid of charitable funding, succeeds to such an extent that the statutory sources take over the work, but can then see that its work is largely done and can pause and contract, while still looking for new, perhaps smaller-scale needs.

Harrow ... the first phase

Sue Sutcliffe

ESL class teaching began in Harrow in 1971 at the instigation of the then principal of Harrow College of Further Education, Mr Joe Hartland.

At that time, the College had been providing EFL classes for about two years, and Mr Hartland decided that specialised provision ought to be made for the ethnic minority population of Harrow. The way he went about this was to hand the matter over to his Section Leader in the Modern Languages Department, Jack Rogers, who was very keen to put the idea into effect. He began to make enquiries and very soon found himself working closely with Ruth Hayman.

It wasn't long before a team of three people was at work teaching the first ESL classes in Harrow. Belinda Ellwood headed the team. She was also setting up the first RSA TEFL course at the College. The other two teachers were Doreen Hilton and Susan Lee.

My own involvement with ESL in Harrow began on Monday, 11th September 1972, the day Jack Rogers interviewed me in the College car park and offered me an evening class at Grant Road Community Centre, Tuesday and Wednesday from 7.15 to 9 p.m., £3.22p per session. I started teaching the same week and I am still at it, over ten years later.

During my first few months of ESL teaching in Harrow enormous expansion took place in the provision of ESL, because it was at this period that refugees began to arrive from Uganda. Ruth was in close and constant touch with the people in the Harrow Community Relations Council who were more closely involved with the refugees, and I was appointed local representative of NEC. With the unfailing support of Jack Rogers, we managed to find premises all over the borough. We opened new community classes in church halls, a synagogue, schools, libraries and a Territorial Army Centre.

All the people recruited to teach these classes were new to

ESL, and I think they would agree that it was extremely stressful to be doing something completely different from anything we had done before, with increasing numbers of students who had recently gone through an appalling experience and whose language needs were desperate.

At first we had to muddle along, adapting EFL techniques and materials. Our great lifeline at this stage was the regular termly NEC seminar, where we received the most fascinating and indispensable basic training.

In 1975 Westminster College launched the RSA Certificate Course in teaching English as a second language to adults, and in the first few years of this course NEC provided a large proportion of the students. Now the vast majority of ESL teachers have taken the RSA course and are in possession of what has become the key qualification for all ESL-related work.

Ruth Hayman features strongly in my memories of the difficult early days of ESL in Harrow. I remember ringing her at all times of the day and night with my problems – a teacher couldn't cope with the noise the students' children were making in the class; a classroom had no blackboard; a class had grown so large that there was no room to squeeze in one more body and now three of the students wanted to bring relatives along; a class had dwindled down to two members; a student was too ill to come to her class any more but desperately wanted English lessons; a student had a child who seemed to have serious behavioural problems – whatever the crisis was, Ruth would come up with a practical suggestion.

It was during this period that classes grew so large that they had to be divided; more and more teachers were recruited and child helpers were appointed. With the arrival of Pamela Frame in the summer of 1975, ESL became a recognised and permanent feature of the Adult Education scene in our borough.

From a handful of classes in 1971, ESL teaching in Harrow has expanded dramatically. We now provide six part-time classes for workseekers; 22 daytime and two evening community classes; a class for mentally handicapped adults in the local Adult Training Centre, and one for physically handicapped adults as well; a 21-hour-per-week Foundation Course for 12 students, and two preparatory TOPS courses for 32 students. We also provide a home tutor service, and offer regular training courses for teachers and home tutors.

How I became a
home tutor organiser

Gul-Anaar Kanji

I came into NEC in a most motherly fashion – as often happened then. I saw an advertisement in my local clinic inviting non-English-speakers wishing to learn English to contact Ruth Hayman.

I had left teaching in schools when I had my first baby. Six months of staying at home and looking after the baby, paying regular visits to the clinic, having weekly coffee mornings with other mothers, had created mental starvation. I longed to get back to teaching.

So I telephoned Ruth to ask if I might teach ESL. She agreed to interview me and on the day arranged she came to meet me at the station and to take me to her house in Lawn Road. I had Shehnaaz in a sling. (Ruth said to me a long time afterwards that it was the baby who had evoked a special warmth in her for me.)

I saw in Ruth a very efficient, very committed and highly intelligent person. Her insistence on the way things should be done was overpowering. Generally she listened, and often she listened for a long time – so that you almost felt that you had lost her, but when she decided to respond her remarks were penetrating and her grasp of what you had said almost unnerving as she saw beyond your words.

I was taken on as a volunteer at one of the local evening classes, and then as a teacher. For two or three years I taught classes in Brent, until I was appointed home tutor organiser in Harrow in June 1975, after the NEC application for urban aid was successful.

Well, the newly-appointed home tutor organiser was well and truly pregnant, and my second baby was due in September/ October, when it was understood that I would take maternity leave. It was decided that for the next three months I would meet as many key people in Harrow as possible. This I did, and I remember many expressive faces silently remarking on my condition.

From the very start, great importance was placed on NEC working with the organisations and groups in the borough. Contact was made with libraries, clinics, churches, social services, employment offices, local voluntary bureaux and so on. It is this level of work which has expanded and grown more complex in Harrow, and the initial relationships have deepened.

Every year there were new developments and new challenges. No project, no idea was turned down without investigation. The home tutor scheme maintains a roll of about 50 students at present, and exists to support the main provision of ESL classes which over the years have proliferated like mushrooms. Referrals for home students poured in from newly-found friends in various organisations.

The Harrow ESL scheme matured and became one of the leading schemes in the country. With maturity came an ever-growing commitment from Harrow College of Further Education. Pamela Frame, who became leader of the ESL section at the College in 1975, began to emerge as the main architect of the scheme as it stands now.

It is wonderful to look back on those days when there were stresses and strains. Friends and colleagues who seemed to be very distant and a bit cold at times were somehow good friends – sensitive to one another's feelings, supportive and kind, encouraging and helpful.

Our English language scheme is now part of the borough and is consulted by anyone wishing to know more about our ethnic minorities. During my eight years in the scheme I have seen it change from a 'recruiting campaign' to a large, sophisticated and most professional set-up.

My energies have been devoted very much to working with our local communities and developing their awareness that we are all part of the whole community of Harrow.

Child helpers

Sandra Cheetham

I

How well I remember Gul-Anaar's telephone call on a dismal January day with the snow falling outside and my son inside regularly being sick with whooping-cough. Did I have a couple of hours to spare each week to help set up an exciting new playgroup scheme for the children of mothers coming to ESL classes in Harrow?

My experiences as a home tutor had not completely prepared me for the daunting task which lay ahead; in fact, I don't think I would have said yes if I'd known just how daunting it would sometimes prove to be. Nevertheless, five years later I look at the flourishing Child Helper Schemes in Hackney, Islington and Watford, and wonder how it all came about.

In the early days I had the wonderful support of Gul-Anaar, Joyce Thomas, Annie Millet and, of course, Ruth herself, who was entirely committed to the cause of the child within NEC. Indeed, Ruth always objected to the use of the term 'crèche' to describe our work with children, for she maintained that we were not providing a child-minding service but were actively helping the pre-school child's development.

Gradually we evolved a recruiting and training programme, decided after bitter experience what were the best and most durable toys for our limited premises and had regular meetings to monitor our progress. Not long after my appointment we acquired two more child helper organisers when Sabrina in Hackney and Sue in Islington and Haringey joined our ranks.

Although we do not attempt to teach the children who come to us in a formal way, we do encourage them to learn through play activities like those they will encounter in nursery, playgroup or infant school. As most of the community classes are themselves camping out in church halls and clinics, we cannot offer the full range of activities to be found in the ordinary playgroup or nursery. Also, we do have a wider age-range, because we

85

encourage mothers to bring their babies as soon as they feel able to come to classes.

Of course, it is the personality of the child helper herself that determines the success of any group, and we have been really fortunate in the band of totally committed women who have taken on this valuable and difficult work. Sylvia, Hansa, Jyoti, Sisko, have been with us from the very beginning and they and their colleagues' contributions to the enrichment of many toddlers' pre-school experiences cannot be measured. Indeed, although we may never see the fruits of our labours, several teachers have commented that they can always tell the children who have had some play experience with NEC.

We have had our fun times, too, many parties and summer projects with our own children joining in. At our most recent Christmas party in Brent, in December 1982, in the midst of the hilarity with Father Christmas giving the excited children their presents, I wished Ruth could have been with us to see so many happy faces and the fruition of many of our hopes.

We have come a long way since we realised that mothers would bring their children with them to our classes and we should really be providing them with something constructive to do. Now in Harrow we have 'crêche' facilities at all 12 of our community classes, and Brent has 22 with the potential for more if funds were available.

One of the most interesting new ventures is the Milan Club, four of which have been started in Brent this year. 'Milan' means *coming together* or *meeting* in more than one Asian language, and the idea behind these clubs is to encourage women of any age or nationality to meet together and plan for themselves what they would like to do. English is not taught in any formal way, but outside speakers and topics of interest to anyone living in North West London in the 1980s are part of the programme of the clubs. In this way we hope that we are reaching and encouraging women who may not necessarily want to learn English in a class, but who do feel isolated at home and have perhaps not yet found outside contacts.

II

In November 1981, Brent NEC applied for urban aid funding for its work with children through the child helper scheme. Here is the outline we prepared to show the purpose, scope and the need for expansion of this work:

The Child Helper Scheme
in
Neighbourhood English
Classes

Mothers with pre-school children are encouraged to bring them to those daytime community classes where there are facilities for their care while their mothers are learning English.

These are not merely crèche facilities, for we employ qualified play-group leaders to introduce the children to the concepts of learning through play which they will encounter on entry to playgroup or school. We do not attempt to teach the children English in any formal way, but we use the play equipment and introduce activities they will meet in playgroup and school so that they may become familiar with them. These include, for example, cutting and sticking, painting and water play, doing puzzles and other activities which they are unlikely to be familiar with at home.

In many cases, the visit to the NEC class is one of the few regular contacts with the English environment a pre-school child and its mother will have outside the home. Because of her linguistic handicap, the non-English-speaking mother is unable to take full advantage of the facilities available to her. She cannot find the words to express sufficiently the problems she may be having with her child at the clinic or answer her health visitor's questions adequately. She may not be aware of the play-groups available to her child or the procedure for enrolment. Still less is she able to combat her isolation and pluck up her courage to go to a local mother/toddler club to meet her peers for a friendly chat, as she is totally lacking in confidence and the ability to make small talk.

Far away from the support of the extended family to which she is used, she is imprisoned in her isolation and her pre-school children likewise lack the opportunity to meet and play with others.

It is, therefore, with great care that we recruit helpers to look after the children who come to us. Wherever possible, women representing the ethnic minorities residing in Brent are employed. They are a vital bridge between the communities, since they have themselves encountered the problems our mothers are facing. They are able to advise and help, very often where necessary in the mother tongue. They are able to judge when a mother or child needs specialist help or when a friendly word of reassurance will solve the problem. Thus, coming to the classes fulfills, to a certain extent, a social as well as a linguistic need. At the present time we have Gujerati, Punjabi, West Indian, Italian and Irish-speaking women working with us as child helpers.

Since 1978, the provision for pre-school children in our classes has grown to cover twelve locations, usually providing two sessions of two hours each a week. The team of child helpers is led by a child helper adviser, who provides the support and co-ordination necessary to keep the scheme running smoothly. She is also responsible for recruiting and training new staff and arranging regular meetings and seminars.

We are, at present, because of financial restrictions, unable to expand the scheme, although we are aware that we only cater for 60-70 under-5s who do not have English as their first language. Considering the ethnic population of Brent, we are reaching only the tip of the iceberg.

If expansion were possible, we should be able to extend the provision of child care sources and recruit more mothers with pre-school children. More self-help projects – such as mother/toddler groups, English for pregnancy – could be implemented, as well as extending the liaison with the health and social services etc. to cultivate awareness of the problems which linguistically handicapped mothers and children are facing.

NEC and the Chinese community

Victor Chan

The teaching of English to the Chinese community in London started from a modest beginning of one class in 1971 to the present number of ten (1983). Throughout these years, numerous restaurant workers, housewives and even students have benefited from these classes. Much of the credit is due to the foresight and sagacity of one person – Mrs Ruth Hayman.

Language barrier was long recognised as one of the major set-backs for the Chinese community in their integration into society at large. In recognition of this vital need, Mrs Ruth Hayman took the initiative to arrange English classes for the Chinese community. It was in 1971 when the first English class began that the Hong Kong Government Office in London started to co-operate with the NEC in the running of classes by contributing partial funds. A happy and cordial working relationship has been established since then.

Mrs Hayman was actively involved with NEC in the Chinatown area, often seeing to the classes personally. Her dedication and unflagging spirit motivated many others to follow suit.

With such keen effort and generous support from the NEC, English classes soon found solid ground in the Chinatown area. In mid-1979, these classes were transferred under the aegis of the Central Institute of Adult Education of the Inner London Education Authority, and continue to flourish up to now.

And the valuable and fruitful contribution of Mrs Ruth Hayman is long remembered by the Chinese community.

Hong Kong Government Office,
London.

Evolution and devolution in Brent

John Fitzpatrick

A minor explosion in ESL for adults in Brent over the past three years has propelled the number of classes held each week from 30 to 67 (September 1983).

Our students range from beginners to examination level, and now we have 'link-skilled' as well as special ESL/literacy classes – that is, classes in cookery and English language, sewing and English language, etc. Around 20 of our daytime classes have qualified child helpers for the students' pre-school children, and a very recent development has been the inauguration of four Milan clubs for mothers and their toddlers. Spoken English is an essential ingredient of these friendly get-togethers.

Our students are referred to us by their relatives and neighbours, by job centres, social and community workers, ethnic minority groups and so on. That the local demand is substantial can be seen from the fact that during one year we received 900 referrals!

Brent, an outer borough of north-west London, has one of the highest ratios of ethnic minority residents in the country. Estimates put at over 30,000 the number of adults for whom English is their second language.

From the arrival of NEC in Brent and in its subsequent endeavours and achievements, the local authority has given more than a helping hand. It has provided the funds for teaching, accommodation and administration. Many local councillors have been alert to local needs and have helped us on our way with their encouragement and commitment.

Relationships of mutual benefit have been built up with many of our borough's voluntary and statutory bodies – the Brent Council for Community Relations, ethnic minority organisations, the police, the libraries, the fire brigade, health, social and community services, the schools and other educational establishments – the list of enthusiastic and helpful organisations and individuals is a long one.

Some of our teachers were with us in the early days and are with us still: Noel Witheford, Jane Siegel, Nora Gutmann, Cathy Galashan, Zakia Bhutt. One of our teachers, Kumud Banarse, has taken on the job of part-time home tutor organiser.

Other members of our team, all part-time workers, are Mary Heywood, Brent NEC's administrative assistant; Sandra Cheetham, child helper adviser; and Daljit Ahluwahlia, in charge of the Milan clubs. How we have managed to cope with the seemingly inexhaustible demands made upon our services remains a mystery. Ability, and loyalty, and a sense of humour – yes. But without the keenness and steadfastness of our students, teachers and volunteer workers, and the co-operation of organisations throughout our borough, our work would not have flourished. Without the counsel of NEC chairman, Ruth Hayman, and later of Frances Weinreich, and of their fellow executive committee members, we might at times have found ourselves in a pretty pickle!

Now the first page of a new chapter has been turned. From April 1983 Brent Council assumed full responsibility for our work and, alongside the Brent Adult Education Project, we are part of the Basic Skills Unit of Brent Education Department.

Our new name is Brent Neighbourhood English Scheme.

Coherent, comprehensive and complementary

Pam Frame

Over the past ten years Harrow, an outer London borough, has developed a comprehensive range of ESL provision. All the ESL work for adults has been brought under the main administrative unit, and this has proved to be a tremendous advantage in organising a coherent programme, in recruiting and referring students effectively and in ensuring communication and co-operation between staff members.

The early work was initiated by Neighbourhood English Classes who persuaded Harrow College of Further Education to set up several community-based part-time classes.

This joint venture has flourished as the Harrow ESL Scheme and now provides part-time classes for the unemployed, community classes with child helpers so that mothers of young children can attend, a class for mentally handicapped adults and another for the physically handicapped, a half-time course for the young unemployed and home based one-to-one tuition as well as training for home tutor volunteers.

In any one term, the Scheme reaches – and teaches – from four to five hundred local residents from overseas. Most of our students are Gujerati-speaking Asians, although other students of Asian origin, Chinese, or Japanese, are also well represented.

From this community-based programme the College has developed complementary provision as part of the scheme, such as the two preparatory TOPS courses which cater almost exclusively for students of ethnic minority origin; a 21-hour foundation course for the young unemployed; and a range of RSA teacher-training courses.

Staff have recently become involved in 'racism awareness' and communications training for local authority and hospital employees, and are initiating a college-wide 'language across the curriculum' project to support second-language speakers who are

93

attending mainstream courses.

All the staff who teach ESL in Harrow have been funded through Section 11 urban aid, or the training division of the Manpower Services Commission, and this has enabled the work to grow without the local authority having to meet additional costs.

We have also benefited from the good support and strong commitment of senior college staff.

Every penny did the work of two

Hazel Scarr

It will be obvious to all who read this history of NEC how much has been achieved by – and indeed would have been impossible without – volunteers. Largely due to these tireless, enthusiastic, but unpaid people the original small pilot projects grew and flourished, until eventually regular funding became essential. NEC had therefore to find sources of income to continue and enlarge its work – the rapid growth of which served to prove the very real need which existed, and which it sought to fill.

Anyone who knew Ruth Hayman will know that she was an indefatigable fund-raiser – some say a 'hell raiser'! – and many a strong man quaked when met by her with a request for money. However, her infectious enthusiasm for what she believed in persuaded a wide variety of very different sources to contribute to the work. These ranged from individuals to large trusts and foundations, and their response was always heartwarming. This is not meant to be a complete chronicle of every financial contribution received, but we should mention by name the larger trusts whose generosity over the years of setting up the major schemes was invaluable. The Allen Lane Foundation gave £14,000 over the years from 1972 to 1980; City Parochial Trust gave £23,100 from 1972 to 1979, and the Noel Buxton Trust gave £18,000 from 1976 to 1982. Many others gave generously, some for specific smaller projects, some in general support, and throughout Ruth made sure that every penny did the work of two.

These were the years in which the main aim was to prove the need to the local authorities. Once able to enlist their support we could apply for funding through urban aid grants, which gave a more permanent backing, usually for an initial five-year term, which could then be renewed. NEC often made a joint application with the local Community Relations Council, alongside which it always tried to work. Results were gradual, some areas being quicker to take up the work than others, but gradually success came. In Camden and Harrow, grant aid came in support of the home tutor schemes set up by NEC. In Hackney and Islington grant aid funds were made available through the Inner City Partnership for the child helper schemes developed by NEC in support of the classes. Some areas were more difficult to crack, but Ruth never missed an opportunity to lobby some unsuspecting councillor, and eventually even the seemingly impossible doors opened. Urban aid was granted for Barnet based on the home tutor scheme, for Watford based on a child helper scheme, and a joint application for child helper and home tutor schemes in Brent was approved. We must mention here the contribution made by the Commission for Racial Equality who on a number of occasions made up 'bridging' grants for one year only in order to keep projects going while NEC continued its fight for more permanent support. This was invaluable, especially in Barnet and Watford.

Ruth also campaigned strongly for 'unseen' funds – that is, to get local authorities to spend some of their own money in support of the work. Her notable success here, after constant bombardment of the members of the Education Department, was the agreement of Brent to create a full-time Language Organiser post, and then second the person to NEC to work with the executive committee.

NEC's ultimate aim was to 'get the show on the road' and then hand over to the local authority, and this has already been achieved in several areas. In Camden, Hackney, Islington and Brent, the local authority now run all aspects of the language scheme including classes, home tutors, and child helpers. In Barnet the administration of the urban aid has been taken over by the Co-ordinating Committee, and the work is slowly expanding while seeking its own additional funding. Harrow and Watford run all their own classes, and Watford runs its own home tutor scheme, but the other aspects are still administered under urban aid by NEC. Transfer of this administration is currently being discussed.

Alongside these major projects small spin-off schemes inevitably arose. In Harrow there was a need for a meeting place for the Asian community, and this was set up at the Kenmore Community Centre. A grant from the CRC followed NEC's pilot project and subsequently the local police charity fund made a generous contribution. In Brent money has been obtained from the local authority to set up and run mother and toddler groups. Small one-off projects have been funded by NEC, of which a prime example was *Beating the Language Barrier*, a course devised to help workers in the health service communicate more effectively with patients with little or no English.

Currently, NEC has various ideas for the use of its remaining funds. These include supporting the development of mother and toddler clubs in both Brent and Barnet; planning and producing a video cassette for training home tutors, providing more tape recorders, producing a demonstration tape, and putting together Home Tutor Resource Packs.

For all those who have contributed financially to NEC's work, from the students' bring and buy sales in their classrooms, to the trusts and foundations who made large donations, the spread and continuation of the original brain-child of Ruth Hayman into the large local language-schemes of today, must be their greatest reward. It has been a privilege to be part of that work.

NEC and NATESLA

Sheila Rosenberg

My first meeting with Ruth Hayman was at the United Kingdom Asian Women's Conference in, I think, 1976. Watching her knit her way imperturbably through a delivery by David Lane, the newly appointed chairman of the CRE, I think I understood right from the first that her impassivity marked a passionate commitment to the theme of the conference, finding and using a voice for Asian women, not on their behalf, but alongside them.

I already knew of her, of course, starting as I had as a volunteer in the Wandsworth Language Scheme with Margaret Hinchcliffe and hearing of the work of the other pioneers of ESL in London. Ruth's name was mentioned constantly. In those days the Commission for Racial Equality played an important role in creating links between language schemes, and in August 1976 it published a list of language teaching schemes in Great Britain. NEC headed the list for London with the unambiguous statement:

> NEC classes are held for adult immigrants in this country.
> Functional everyday English is taught to enable students to
> communicate in situations where English is needed.

It is followed by a list of boroughs in which NEC operated, indicating the range of their activities. It was this combination of the practical expertise necessary to finance, set up and run an organisation and the firm underlying commitment to redressing the imbalance and providing opportunities for immigrants, especially women and their young children, that Ruth, via NEC, was to contribute to the further development of ESL in the UK, particularly the establishment of NATESLA.

With a reputation among ESL schemes already so firmly established and consolidated, it was inevitable that Ruth would be one of the first organisers to be invited to the BBC *Parosi*

98

seminar for the South, at Garnett College, Roehampton, in July 1977. The BBC's two national seminars, North and South, were attended by representatives of a great many of the language schemes listed by the CRE, and reflected Community Relations Councils, voluntary and LEA funded schemes.

The aim of the seminars was to discuss plans for the BBC's new English Language teaching programme. Looking at the seminar programme and my hastily scribbled notes, I am struck again by the remarkable consensus among all present on who the client group was and how their needs should be met. The BBC spokesman referred to the finding of the PEP report, *The Facts of Racial Disadvantage* (1976), that 59 per cent of Asian women in the UK spoke little or no English. This assertion came as no surprise to organisers working in schemes like NEC who had already established that particular combination of home tuition and small community classes aimed especially at meeting the language needs of Asian women. Michael Mobbs had first (April 1977) characterised in some detail the work of schemes in many parts of the country in the CRC publication, *Meeting their Needs, an Account of Language Tuition Schemes for Ethnic Minority Women*, in which it is very clear again that the main group of women being catered for were from the Indian subcontinent and East Africa.

The seminars, therefore, only confirmed the BBC in their intention to develop further a programme of tuition of a similar kind and for the same group as was already being provided across the country.

There was, however, one major and unforeseen result of the two seminars. Organisers from all over the country were able to meet in two large groups for the first time. Until then national co-ordination of schemes had been undertaken by the CRC and CRE on the basis of local area meetings. Now at these two seminars, separately, there was unanimous agreement on the value of national contacts and meetings, and the decision was taken to set up a national association.

An ad hoc working party of representatives from the two seminars was set up, chaired by Judith Sanson of the Hammersmith CRC scheme, to plan the inaugural meeting of the new association. From the beginning Ruth was an active member and we drew on her experience of founding organisations, drafting constitutions and planning means of securing funding. She was largely responsible for preparing a draft constitution and also briefed herself on the feasibility of

99

charitable status for the new organisation.

The founding meeting took place on 25 February 1978 in Birmingham. The sessions were chaired by Robbie Robinson, vice-chairman of the CRE. Delegates were greeted by Dan Cook on behalf of the BBC, and HMI Eric Bolton, who had responsibility for multi-cultural education, spoke in the opening session. He emphasised the need for much more comprehensive and co-ordinated ESL provision, much better funded and with LEAs playing a much fuller role. Sandra Nicholls of the ILEA then presented a stirring overview of the future of ESL to meet a range of diversifying needs and responsibilities, and develop through adult and further education to provide for students of different ages and backgrounds, far beyond the range of provision that had been possible so far. Adèle Attwood from Bradford concluded the morning programme with a vivid picture of the reality of patchy, underfunded provision existing at that time.

By lunchtime therefore the new association had already both faced the inadequacies and problems of current ESL provision and also firmly grasped the need not only to improve what was already being done, but the importance of moving on to meet the needs of different client groups in a variety of ways.

In the afternoon business meeting another important change occurred. The initial proposal had been for a National Association of English Language Schemes, with the appropriately doughty acronym of NAELS. At Ruth's suggestion, on behalf of the steering group, this was now discarded because it was decided that individual membership was much preferable. It would get over the problem of defining 'language schemes', allow for individual freedom of choice and ensure a much wider representation of teachers from all sectors – voluntary schemes, paid provision in adult and further education, industrial language training units – all uniting in a National Association for Teaching English as a Second Language to Adults.

Ruth then spoke on the possibility of obtaining charitable status for the new organisation so that funding would be much easier. The meeting mandated a Provisional National Council to explore this. The proposal that the association should be run by a provisional executive council of two members from each of nine regions was passed unanimously and the other clauses of the constitution were remitted to the next general meeting.

The first meeting of the Provisional National Council took place in April 1978. Ruth became Honorary Secretary and continued so until her death in October 1981.

It was characteristic of Ruth that, while remaining totally committed to what NEC stood for, she immediately understood the need for a wider and more political base for the new national association. She never lost sight of the value of volunteer work and of the paramount importance of building trust and understanding among communities in a multi-racial society, but she also understood that there are other groups needing tuition and other ways of providing it. From early on she understood the needs of 16-19-year-olds and the newly unemployed, both of whose disadvantages grew as the recession deepened. She was particularly aware of the position of newly-arrived refugees from South America and South East Asia, some of whom were provided for through NEC.

It was this capacity to see what was needed in a changing world, as well as her understanding of organisational structures, her legal training and her persuasive canvassing of support that NATESLA drew on. She had an enormously wide range of contacts.

So, from the drawing up of the NATESLA constitution which was ratified at the next general meeting, and again in Birmingham in October 1978 and through all the subsequent conferences, delegations and other activities of the association, she was at the centre. She worked as tirelessly for NATESLA as she continued to do for NEC. We could benefit from her energy, expertise and experience, but we gained above all from her conviction that we should aim high and be satisfied with nothing less than the most effective and efficient organisation possible.

Probably both a lasting testament to her, and the last work she did for NATESLA, is embodied in the charity that now bears her name. After that first mandate in February 1978 to explore the possibility of charitable status she worked relentlessly. She accepted initial expert opinion that NATESLA itself did not qualify for charitable status, especially as she saw one of the vital roles for the new organisation as that of a pressure group, able to act independently and freely. She therefore sought legal advice on establishing a separate organisation that would satisfy the Charity Commissioners. Most of this work she did alone, reporting back to the Management Council on her progress, presenting drafts of constitutions, asking for our opinion.

In the month she died, we received news that we might finally be successful. At the annual conference in Brighton the following month there was a unanimous decision to set up a trust fund in her memory, and when the details of the new charitable organisation were finalised, the two were united in the Ruth Hayman Memorial Trust.

As treasurer of the Trust I have been made vividly aware of the range of well-wishers from business, industry, the legal and academic worlds, voluntary organisations, those involved in working for good community relations and against racism, individual organisers, teachers, volunteers, students, all wanting to pay tribute to Ruth.

This ability to draw on and keep such a range of support is what Ruth brought to NEC and NATESLA alike and is a tribute to her energy and her ability to take others with her. But the range also bears testimony to the way she realised the need to change and adapt as changing needs and situations presented themselves. This is clearly seen in comparing NATESLA and NEC. NATESLA differs from NEC not just in size but in concept. The members come from a range of providing bodies, showing LEAs rightly taking an increasing responsibility for second language speakers of all ages and backgrounds, and the organisation properly plays a national role in lobbying central government on a widening range of issues affecting ESL speakers and the funding of provision.

So finally, if I am to assess the contribution of NEC to NATESLA, I would point first to the fact that it was a powerful pioneer in the field of ESL tuition especially to women, and therefore played a major role in creating that consciousness and understanding out of which the new organisation could grow. But I would also point to it as initial evidence of Ruth Hayman's ability to identify and make provision for the needs of second language speakers in the UK, needs which grew, evolved and diversified and then needed a wider, national and more political organisation which became a second testament to her energy and vision.

Abbreviations

AEI	Adult Education Institute
CCCR	Camden Committee for Community Relations
CCSS	Camden Council of Social Services
CRC	Community Relations Council
CRE	Commission for Racial Equality
EFL	English as a Foreign Language
ESL	English as a Second Language
HMI	Her Majesty's Inspector (of Schools)
ILEA	Inner London Education Authority
LEAs	Local Education Authorities
NATESLA	National Association for Teaching English as a Second Language to Adults
NAC	Neighbourhood Advice Centre
PATHWAY	Original name for scheme subsequently called National Industrial Training Unit
PEP	Political and Economic Planning – a research group
RSA	Royal Society of Arts – functions as an examining body for a variety of skills including language teaching
TEFL	Teaching English as a Foreign Language
TESL	Teaching English as a Second Language, usually to immigrants
TOPS	Training Opportunities Programme
URBAN AID	Grant aid for deprived inner city areas
VOSA	Volunteer Overseas Service Agency

Class List for the Autumn Term 1973

By the autumn of 1973, NEC was administering and teaching students in more than 40 classes in and around London. Sometimes more than one class was held in the same venue.

Classes in Brent were conducted in association with the Brent Education Department and in Camden, with the Camden Committee for Community Relations, Marylebone Institute and Paddington College for Further Education. In Ealing we worked in conjunction with the Ealing Education Authority and in Hackney with the Highbury Manor Institute and the Hackney Community Relations Council.

Haringey classes were run in association with the Haringey Education Department and in Harrow with the Harrow College of Further Education. There were special workseeker classes in Wealdstone that year for Ugandan Asians. In Islington classes were run in association with the Islington Committee for Community Relations and the Holloway Institute.

Classes in Kensington were in association with the Kensington Institute and in Westminster with the Central London Institute and the Hong Kong Government Office.

The following list is broken down into areas and individual schools where classes were held, the names of the teachers in attendance appear in italics.

Brent:
Harlesden Methodist Church, NW10 *Jean Wright*
St Michael's Church, Wembley *Gul-Anaar Kanji*
Methodist Church, Wembley (2 classes) *Betty Jacobs and Nora Gutmann*
Sudbury Baptist Church, Sudbury *Nora Gutmann*
Alperton High School, Wembley *Alan Fisher*
Copland High School, Wembley *M.T. Narale*
Anson Road School, NW2 *Jan Malden*
Furness Road School, NW10 *Halima Bellows*
Gladstone Park School, NW10 (2 classes) *Simon Buckland and Nora Gutmann*
John Kelly School, NW2 *Jean Wright*
Kilburn Square Family Welfare Clinic, NW6 *Elizabeth Tinker*
Kinsbury High School, NW9 (2 classes) *Honor Nettleton and Barbara Spiro*

Camden:
Gospel Oak Family Welfare Clinic, NW5   *Shirin Spencer*
The Health Centre, Bartholomew Villas, NW5   *Frances Weinreich*
St Cuthbert's Church, NW6   *Elizabeth MacDonald*
Minster Road Day Nursery, NW6   *Shirin Spencer*
Haverstock Comprehensive School, NW3   *Sara Wood*

Ealing:
Tudor Park Junior School, Southall, Middlesex   *Kay Levans*

Hackney:
Clissold Park School, N16 (2 classes)   *Judy Deeks and Beverley Sedley*
St Mary's Church Hall, N16   *Gillian Frost*

Haringey:
St Peter's Hall, N8   *Shirley Sadler Forster*

Harrow:
Congregational Church   *Helen Hodges*
Vaughan Road School   *Kumud Kothari*
Grant Road School (2 classes)   *Audrey D'Avray and Helen Hughes*
Glebe School, Kenton   *Ralph Salinger*
Camrose School, Edgware   *Julia Merrick*
Grant Road School (2 classes for workseekers)   *Belinda Ellwood and Sue Sutcliffe*

Islington:
North Islington Welfare Centre, N7   *Fiona Dobbs*
Barnsbury Clinic, N1   *Jane Moyes*
Family Welfare Centre, Drayton Park, N1   *Mary Eyton*

Kensington:
Walmer Road Health Centre, W10   *Gayle Secretan*

Westminster:
4 Gerrard Street, W1   *Vera Miles*
16 Old Compton Street, W1   *Patricia Moynagh*

By 1979, the class list was considerably expanded. Classes were being held not only in the boroughs listed above, but in Barnet, Hillingdon, Luton and Watford. NEC was involved in the teaching of over 118 classes in that year.

Executive Committee Members

The following served as members of the committee at different periods from 1970 to the present:

Usha Bagri
Kumud Banarse
Marjorie Beadle
Margaret Beard
Esther Blackburn
Louise Child
Jaya Chouhan
Belinda Ellwood
John Fitzpatrick
Rose Grant
Krystyna Gunderman
Nora Gutmann
Katherine Hallgarten
Ruth Hayman (chairman, 1970-1981)

Ann Herschmann
Lucy Jonckheere
Gul-Anaar Kanji
Joyce Morton
Patience Robb
Shirley Sadler Forster
Elaine Self
Indu Sheth
Joyce Thomas
Elizabeth Tinker
Diana Townsend
Frances Weinreich (chairman, 1981-present)
Sara Wood
Sue Zagor

by invitation: Sandra Cheetham, Susan Hunt, Caroline Iffla Romijn, Hazel Scarr

This History was designed by
Derek Doyle and prepared for
the press by Deborah Blake.
Penny Phillips did the lettering
and Sasha Devas designed the cover.

Our thanks to them and to the
following suppliers for helpful
advice and generous support:

Derek Doyle & Associates
Redwood Burn Ltd
Cylinder Typesetting Ltd
and Cylinder Press Ltd